The Role of Social Work in Poverty Reduction and Realization of MDGs in Kenya

The Role of Social Work in Poverty Reduction and Realization of Millennium Development Goals in Kenya

By

Gidraph G. Wairire
Agnes P. Zani
Mumbi Machera
Pius M. Mutie

University of Nairobi Press

Austrian
Development Cooperation

appear

Austrian Partnership Programme
in Higher Education and Research
for Development

First published 2014 by
University of Nairobi Press (UONP)
Jomo Kenyatta Memorial Library
University of Nairobi
P.O. Box 30197 – 00100 Nairobi
E-mail: nup@uonbi.ac.ke | www.uonbi.ac.ke/press

The University of Nairobi Press supports and promotes University of Nairobi's objectives of discovery, dissemination and preservation of knowledge, and stimulation of intellectual and cultural life by publishing works of the highest quality in association with partners in different parts of the world. In doing so, it adheres to the University's tradition of excellence, innovation and scholarship.

University of Nairobi Library CIP Data

Wairire, Gidraph *et al*

HV 11.8

.K4W3

The role of social work in poverty reduction and realization of millennium development goals in Kenya / by G. Wairire *et al*. – Nairobi: University of Nairobi Press, 2014

155p.

1. Social service – Kenya 2. Kenya – Economic conditions
3. Kenya – Social conditions   I. Title

ISBN 10: 9966-792-52-X

ISBN 13: 978-9966-792-52-5

Printed by

ALIKI Printers and Stationers Limited
P.O. Box 51762-00200
Nairobi, Kenya

Table of Contents

List of Tables

List of Figures

About the Authors

Dr. Gidraph G. Wairire is a Senior Lecturer in the Department of Sociology and Social Work, University of Nairobi. He holds a PhD in Social Work, Master of Arts in Social Work and BSW (Bachelor of Social Work). He served as the Kenya country coordinator and the regional coordinator of the PROSOWO Project (2011–2014). His main interests include social work theory and practice, community development, counseling, international social work, developmental social work, social work with minorities, comparative sociology and social action for social change. His scholarly work has been published as book chapters and journal articles and he has presented papers in international conferences and symposia.

Dr. Agnes P. Zani is currently on secondment to the Senate of Kenya, has been a Lecturer at the University of Nairobi since 1993. She holds PhD in Sociology, MA in Sociology and Bachelor of Arts in Sociology. She has been involved in the teaching, supervising and mentoring of students training to be sociologists and social workers. She served as a senior researcher in the PROSOWO Project. Her main areas of focus and interest have been professionalizing social work, professional ethics in Kenyan careers, gender and education, culture and social change, human resources management and social statistics. She has authored over twenty articles and published in referred journals.

Dr. Mumbi Machera is a Lecturer in the Department of Sociology and Social Work, University of Nairobi. She holds a PhD in Sociology, a Master of Arts Degree in Population Studies and a Bachelor of Arts Degree in Social Work. She served as a senior researcher in the PROSOWO Project. She is also a Gender and Development Specialist, working closely with academic institutions as well as local and international development agencies in pursuit of gender equality goals.

The late **Dr. Pius M. Mutie** was a Senior Lecturer in the Department of Sociology and Social Work, University of Nairobi. He held a PhD in Social Anthropology and Development Sociology, a Master of Arts in Sociology and a Bachelor of Arts in Social Work. He also served as a senior researcher in the PROSOWO Project. His academic interests included natural resource management, social welfare, social development, and family and child welfare. He died of cancer in 2013 while the writing of this book was in progress and made significant contributions to the draft manuscript.

Foreword

The training of professional social workers in Kenya can be traced to the then Israel School of Social Work in the early 1960s which was initially based at Machakos but later on assimilated into the Kenya Institute of Administration, Kabete. In the late 1970s, the Department of Sociology of the University of Nairobi started its Bachelor of Arts degree programme in social work. In late 1990s, the department started a diploma programme in social work and social development. Since then, social work training programmes have been started by other institutions such as Daystar and Masinde Muliro Universities, and by a large number of middle-level colleges. These programmes have attracted a large number of students.

The goal of the social work training has been to produce graduates who can fit in various challenging roles in Kenya, and today social workers occupy critical positions in various institutions throughout the country.

The training, among other things, equips trainees with sufficient know-how and skills for working with needy groups and individuals, more particularly the poor and very poor who have been a concern for the country since independence. Various sessional papers, development plans and other policy documents have emphasized eradication of poverty. Despite this, poverty has persisted and worsened in the 1990s with an estimated 56 per cent of Kenyans falling below the poverty line owing to the poor performance of the economy at the time. Since then, there has been considerable improvement in the performance of the economy and it is now estimated that 46 per cent of Kenyans fall below the poverty line. The improvement has resulted from various policies and programmes such as: the Economic Recovery Strategy of 2003; the establishment of several devolved funds, for example, the Constituency

Development Fund (CDF); and the Kenya Vision 2030 and its associated programmes that have enabled communities to construct facilities, access services and engage in livelihood activities towards meeting the Millennium Development Goals (MDGs).

Social workers at various levels of society have contributed in the formulation, planning and implementation of policies and programmes. Despite this contribution there has been no concerted effort made to examine and document the effort and associated impact. Likewise, there has been no reflection on various aspects of social work training, namely: review of the syllabus, quality assurance, student field placement and internship, student enrolment, and more importantly assessment of the training in the performance of social work graduates in various agencies, and contribution to the economy at large.

The PROSOWO has taken the first big leap toward understanding of the situation of social workers, their training and their contribution to the economy with a focus on poverty reduction and the realization MDGs. Indeed we highly commend PROSOWO efforts to reflect on the training of social workers by meeting and talking to its on-going students and graduates, employer agencies, lecturers and other stakeholders. With more PROSOWO type initiatives in future, the current wide gap in knowledge about training of social workers and their contribution to the economy will be reduced, and the fruitful insights and lessons learnt should enhance visibility of the social work profession.

Preston O. Chitere
Professor of Sociology and Social Work
University of Nairobi

Acknowledgements

Several stakeholders have contributed immensely to the successful completion of this research and the subsequent publication. We shall be eternally beholden to them. Key in this endeavor, is the Austrian Partnership Programme in Higher Education and Research for Development (APPEAR), under the auspices of the Austrian Development Cooperation for financing this study as part of the broad Promotion of Professional Social Work towards Development and Poverty Reduction in East Africa (PROSOWO) Project in the period, February 2011 – November 2014.

We are indebted to Carinthia University of Applied Sciences-Austria that collaborated with the East African partner institutions namely: University of Nairobi-Kenya, Makerere University-Uganda, National University of Rwanda and Institute of Social Work-Tanzania, for the conceptualization, design and implementation of PROSOWO Project in East Africa. In this regard, our profound gratitude goes to Prof. Helmut Spitzer from Carinthia University of Applied Sciences-Austria, the overall PROSOWO project coordinator for his tireless effort and insightful role in coordinating and facilitating the project activities amidst differing social cultural orientations and approaches in our respective regions.

Special thanks go to the entire PROSOWO team comprising Prof. Helmut Spitzer, Dr. Janestic Twikirize, Dr. Zena Mnasi, Mr. Charles Rutikanga - respective country coordinators for Uganda, Tanzania and Rwanda, Ms. Sabrina Riedl from Austria, and all the senior researchers in respective partner countries for their immense contribution in the research design and the formulation of research tools used in this study.

We owe deep gratitude to the research assistants - Mr. Elijah Macharia, Mr. Keith Kiswili, Mr. Eric Onyango and Ms. Elizabeth Mwathi, who played a significant role in collecting the needed information from the respondents in the field. Equally important to mention are the social work practitioners, educators, key informants, social work students from different organizations and institutions who provided the vital data that culminated in this publication.

We are also grateful to the University of Nairobi administration for the facilitative role played at different levels of this research as well as the academic staff in the Department of Sociology and Social Work, for the moral support at different stages of the research process. Our appreciation goes to the University of Nairobi Press for ensuring that the research report was finally published as a book that would greatly fill a critical gap that has existed for years in professional social work education and practice in Kenya. Last but not least, we profoundly appreciate the invaluable inputs of our dear colleague the late Dr. Pius Mutuku Mutie who served as a senior researcher and contributed greatly to the production of this publication but passed on before the publication saw the light of the day. Asanteni sana!

Dr. Gidraph G. Wairire, Dr. Agnes Zani and Dr. Mumbi Machera
Department of Sociology and Social Work - University of Nairobi
November 2014
Nairobi, Kenya

Acronyms

APPEAR	Austrian Partnership Programme in Higher Education and Research for Development
ASAL	Arid and Semi-Arid Lands
CBO	Community Based Organization
CEDAW	Convention on Elimination of All Forms of Discrimination against Women
CUEA	Catholic University of Eastern Africa - Nairobi
DFRD	District Focus for Rural Development
FBO	Faith Based Organization
FGD	Focused Group Discussion
FPE	Free Primary Education
GTI	Government Training Institute
IASSW	International Association of Schools of Social Work
IFAD	International Fund for Agricultural Development
IFSW	International Federation of Social workers
KISW	Kenya Institute of Social Work
KNBS	Kenya National Bureau of Statistics
KNEC	Kenya National Examination Council
MDG	Millennium Development Goals
MSW	Masters in Social Work
MTP	Medium Term Plans
NACC	National Aids Control Council

OVC	Orphaned and Vulnerable Children
PROSOWO	Promotion of Professional Social Work towards Social Development and Poverty Reduction in East Africa
SEUCO	South Eastern University College
SPSS	Statistical Package for Social Sciences
SRDP	Special Rural Development Programme
UNDP	United Nations Development Programme
UON	University of Nairobi
USAID	United States Agency for International Development
WEF	Women Enterprise Development Fund
YEDF	Youth Enterprise Development Fund
UNICEF	United Nations International Children's Emergency Fund
DFID	Department for International Development

Executive Summary

The study that culminated into this publication was part of the Promotion of Professional Social Work towards Social Development and Poverty Reduction in East Africa (PROSOWO) Project, that involved five institutions that offer social work training programmes in East Africa, namely: the University of Nairobi, Makerere University-Uganda, National University of Rwanda, Institute of Social Work-Tanzania, and Carinthia University of Applied Sciences – Austria. The project period run from March 2011 to February 2014 but was extended to November 2014 on a cost neutral base. The project was conceptualized with a research focus on social work in the East African region hence each collaborating institution in East Africa conducted research on the role of social work and its contribution towards poverty reduction in the respective countries.

In Kenya, the research was conducted between September and December 2011 by a team of four senior researchers namely; Dr. Gidraph Wairire, Dr. Agnes Zani, Dr. Mumbi Machera and the late Dr. Pius Mutie, who served as academic staff in the Department of Sociology and Social Work at the University of Nairobi.

Specifically, the purpose of the study was to: appraise the current status of the MDGs, and the challenges faced in achieving the targets in Kenya; identify key programmes undertaken to reduce poverty and enhance social development; determine the extent to which professional social workers are engaged in such programmes; explore the specific roles and tasks undertaken by professional social workers in addressing poverty and the realization of the Millennium Development Goals (MDGs); assess the adequacy of the social work curriculum in preparing social workers to address issues of poverty and MDGs in the country; and analyze cross cutting gender issues related to social work education and practice, and the impact on the effort to address poverty in Kenya.

Research questions focused on the following three main areas: social work education and training; social work practice and other cross cutting issues revolving around policy; and gender, cross cultural and political factors that impact on social work practice in Kenya. The key research questions were: how well social work curricula in Kenya prepare graduates to handle issues of poverty and social development, what specific knowledge and skills they are equipped with, what are the gaps in the social work curriculum, what is the extent to which gender is mainstreamed in the social work curriculum, how does professional social work practice contribute to poverty reduction and achievement of the MDGs in Kenya, and how it address the constraints experienced in the process. Others revolved around the extent to which social development programmes engage social workers, the policy and legal environment for social work education and practice, and what needs to be done to ensure that there is an enabling environment for social work education and practice in Kenya.

A national approach was critical in ensuring appropriate representativeness and coverage hence eight administrative regions in Kenya (previously provinces) were used as a basis for sampling. Multi stage sampling design was therefore adopted and the following four regions: Nairobi, Coast, Eastern and Rift Valley were selected. The study population included social work practitioners, employers in Government and Non Governmental Organizations (NGOs), Community Based Organizations (CBOs) and Faith Based Organizations (FBOs), educators from public and private universities and middle level colleges, final year social work students, clients, and key policy formulators ranging from government ministries to NGO consortiums. Analysis of relevant development documents, applied empirical research through questionnaires, semi-structured interviews, focus group discussions and field visits were used to provide the data analyzed in this report.

Key findings indicate that social workers in Kenya play a very active role in poverty reduction as follows: poverty related problems (68.8%), child neglect (55.4%), food insecurity (26.2%), illiteracy (22.2%), lack of school fees (15.8%), among others. Their intervention activities include economic empowerment (54%), educational support (9.4%), training (7.4%) and provision of basic needs (6.4%) among others. Five per cent of social workers interviewed said they had never heard of MDGs yet social workers are at the epicenter of MDGs realization. However, majority of social workers (56.4%) were aware of MDGs. 83.7 per cent of social workers were aware of the programmes undertaken in Kenya to realize MDGs. There was no particular sector in the MDGs that was not receiving some attention by social workers. Many social workers (76.2%) felt they were in one way or another advancing the global partnership for development agenda. About 67 per cent of social workers indicated that they were involved in eradication of extreme poverty and hunger, 57.4 per cent were involved in a range of health related activities such as improving maternal health, reducing child mortality and combating HIV/AIDs, malaria and other diseases while about 49 per cent were involved in gender empowerment.

With regard to professional training in social work, only 1 per cent of social work practitioners had a master's degree in social work as the highest education qualification. Twenty five per cent had a bachelor's degree in social work, 16 per cent had only a certificate while 8 per cent had other qualifications most probably not in social work. Nonetheless, social work training was found to have sufficiently (57%) prepared the practitioners to work in diverse cultural settings with different client groups. The underlying approach in the current social work curriculum was described by educators as mainly generalist (52.6%), community development approach (36.8%), social development (5.3%) and social planning and administration (5.3%).

Majority of educators (68.4%) indicated that global standards of social work and training were only partly integrated in the curriculum at their institutions of learning while 5.3 per cent indicated that they were not aware of the global standards. Overall only 26.3 per cent asserted that such global standards are fully met in their curriculum. With regard to indigenization of social work, 84.2 per cent of educators asserted that they do contribute to indigenization of social work in Africa. They also pointed out the lack of adequate teaching materials (26.3%), lack of adequate resource materials (21.1%), lack of support from stakeholders (21%), diverse African cultures (15.8%), ideological conflicts (10.5%) and lack of experience on different issues (5.3%) as key challenges for indigenization of social work education and practice in Kenya.

Challenges that confront social work as a profession were found to revolve around training, work environment and the practitioners themselves. These range from the very basic preparations they undergo at the training level, the kind of exposure they get during their field education, the work environment in which they operate on employment, the collegial relationships that determine their professional duties, lack of social work trained personnel with a sound social work knowledge base for different levels of social work training, lack of legislative mechanisms for strong professional body of social workers with a clear mandate to regulate itself and with a clearly defined service delivery process for social work clientele. Sixty eight per cent of social work practitioners indicated they were not aware of any social work association in the country while 32 per cent stated they were. Ninety seven per cent of the respondents indicated they were not members of a national social work association in Kenya while a paltry 3 per cent indicated they were members.

Key recommendations for poverty reduction and realization of MDGs at training level include incorporation of MDGs in social work curriculum, review of social work curriculum to address current social issues, more exposure of social work students on strategies to handle MDG issues, recruitment of more qualified social work lecturers, provision for more social work reference materials, well coordinated field work education for improved integration of social work theory and practice, recognition of social work profession by government, accreditation of social work training institutions, exchange programs with developed countries, more social work research.

Key recommendations for poverty reduction and realization of MDGs at practice level include adoption of MDGs within the structure of agency programmes, recruitment of qualified social work personnel, adherence to professional social work code of ethics, better remuneration of social workers, and government support for social work profession by regulating social work practice and enhancing more indigenized social work interventions.

Key recommendations for poverty reduction and realization of MDGs at policy level include implementation and enforcement of social welfare policies in line with MDGs, involvement of social workers and stakeholders in policy formulation and implementation, professional body to regulate social work practice, consideration of policies that are needs oriented and sustained government support for social work profession.

Although the time span for the implementation of Millennium Development Goals is now almost over, it is hoped that the lessons learnt through this research and the gains made with regard to MDGs should not end with the time span. Social work educators and social work practitioners alike still have more work in making sure that these gains are consolidated in social work training and practice with additional efforts made for their sustainability. This calls for close working relations with all cadres of social workers and streamlining of structures to support such efforts. With regard to the recommendations on social work education, strategies on how to make it more relevant and effective should be worked out and tabled to respective departments and university structures for consideration and ease of implementation. It is also hoped that the Council for University Education in Kenya will consider the recommendations derived through this study in the process of accrediting social work education programmes at university level.

1

Introduction

1.1 Historical Dimensions of Social Work in Kenya

Professional social work education in Kenya dates back to the early 1960's when the training of social work personnel started in earnest at the Kenya Israel School of Social work and later on continued at the Kenya Institute of Administration. The demand for trained social work personnel was quite high immediately after independence in 1963. In order to accelerate social development, the post colonial government realized that political independence was not necessarily the key to direct improvement of people's livelihoods. The local people, in a newly liberated country from colonialism needed more inputs from professionals who could understand their social emotional struggles to rebuild their lives afresh and determine how they would participate in the process, hence the need for trained personnel in social work.

Fifty years since independence from the British, progress in social work education in Kenya has been rather slow. For example, social work training at the University of Nairobi was introduced in 1976 and twenty years later the Catholic University of Eastern Africa started a social work programme in 1996. Other universities have since come up with social work training programmes. These include; Daystar University, Masinde Muliro University of Science and Technology, Maasai Mara University, South Eastern Kenya University and Kibabii University College (constituent college of Masinde Muliro University of Science and Technology). It should nonetheless be noted that other social work training institutions have been training social workers at diploma level since the mid 1960's including the Government Training Institute in Embu and the Kobujoi Institute for Social Development that is run by the Catholic Diocese of Eldoret.

Since 2000, several private commercial colleges have come up in Kenya with training packages for social work at diploma level. The Kenya National Examination Council is the examining body for the social work training offered at this level. Evidently, there is a high unmet demand for trained social work personnel in the country. Professional social work training is expensive hence most institutions are only able to train a small number of students per academic year. A good example is the University of Nairobi that trains between only 80–120 students per year. These constraints are compounded by the fact that trained social work lecturers in public universities are few and with limited opportunities for upward mobility. This is notwithstanding the broad scope of social work in the country that has been changing as the country undergoes different phases of development. Many practitioners have developed fully fledged social work careers in different sectors including child welfare services, probation services, hospital settings, school social work, community development and micro finance institutions (Wairire, 2008).

Besides this, only the Catholic University of Eastern Africa has a postgraduate programme in Social Work, launched in 2012 despite social work training at degree level having started in 1976 in the country. There is little evidence of any studies having been done to explore why this has been the case and why social work education and by extension social work practice seems to be growing at a very slow pace.

Social work as a profession has critical role to play in the reduction of poverty and realization of the United Nations Millennium Goals (MGDs). An assessment of such a role entails a concise research initiative on the role of social work in poverty reduction (Weaver, 2006; Roche, 2004). In view of the above, there is dire need to document the reality on the ground regarding social work professionals and identify the gaps in the following areas: social work curriculum and its application, facilitate social work practice, and suggest appropriate social work initiatives that would address poverty successfully in a gender sensitive approach.

1.2 The PROSOWO Project

The Promotion of Professional Social Work towards Development and Poverty Reduction in East Africa (PROSOWO) project was conceptualized to promote professional social work education and practice within local, regional and international contexts. The project was funded by the Austrian Partnership Programme in Higher Education and Research for Development (APPEAR) within the auspices of the Austrian Development Cooperation. It was a joint initiative of four East African institutions of higher education and one Austrian partner previously mentioned, that combined effort towards regional and international partnerships in promoting social work education.

The project focused on social work research in the East African region. Each partner institution in East Africa conducted research on the role of social work and its contribution towards poverty reduction in their respective country. This was achieved through analysis of relevant development documents and applied empirical research (questionnaires, semi-structured interviews, focus groups, field visits).

The overall objective of the PROSOWO project was to promote professional social work education and practice to contribute effectively towards social development and poverty reduction in achieving the MDGs in East Africa. Specifically, the project aimed at strengthening the capacity of higher education institutions that offer social work in the region through research, curriculum development and joint publications. In addition, the project targeted developing sustainable academic partnerships and networks in Africa and Austria in social work training and research. The project focused on

3

conducting research on the role of social work in poverty reduction towards achieving the MDGs. The research generated empirical data that documented the current status of social work education and practice in partner countries. The project was also meant to develop a more relevant social work curriculum in alignment with national poverty reduction plans and social development strategies, and finally to facilitate the process of drafting a discussion paper on regulating the social work profession for discussions with relevant government authorities.

As earlier mentioned, a major activity towards the realization of this broad objective was the research 'The Role of Professional Social Work in Poverty Reduction and Realization of Millennium Development Goals in East Africa' whose specific objectives were:

1. To appraise the current status of MDGs and the challenges faced in achieving targets in Kenya;

2. To identify key programmes undertaken to reduce poverty and achieve social development, and the extent to which professional social workers are engaged in such programmes;

3. To explore the specific roles and tasks undertaken by professional social workers in addressing poverty and the realization of the MDGs;

4. To assess the adequacy of the social work curriculum in preparing social workers to address issues of poverty and MDGs in the country;

5. To analyze cross cutting gender issues that impact on social work education and practice, that in turn impacts on the efforts to address poverty.

Results of this process yielded four national research reports in the form of books representing each of the four East African countries and one comparative regional research chapter focusing on the critical social work themes prioritized in the study and which was published in the book *Professional social work in East Africa, Towards Social Development, Poverty Reduction and Gender Equality* edited by Helmut Spitzer, Janestic Twikirize and Gidraph Wairire, and revised social work curriculum and scientific papers that were presented in local and international conferences. Most importantly, it was envisaged that the interlinked activities will help improve the capacity of each partner institutions, promote the social work profession, support gender equality, and significantly assist poverty reduction strategies through well-trained and qualified social work staff in each represented country. A major scientific outcome of the whole project is the above mentioned first book on social work in East Africa. The book is a showcase of significant themes and sub-themes on the current state of social work in East Africa.

In Kenya, the research component of the project commenced in September 2011 with a special focus on social work practitioners, educators, clients and students. The study outcomes are expected to contribute to new ideas that may help improve the existing social work curriculum in social work training institutions and also improve the capacities of trained social work professionals in Kenya.

2

Study Methodology and Approaches for Information Gathering

2.1 Introduction

One of the specific objectives of the Promotion of Professional Social Work towards Social Development and Poverty Reduction in East Africa (PROSOWO) project was to conduct research on the role of social work in reduction of poverty and attainment of Millennium Development Goals (MDGs). This entailed exploring specific roles and tasks undertaken by professional social workers and how they impact on social development. To achieve this, the information on the roles played was obtained from different stakeholders who included social work practitioners, educators, policy makers, students and even the clients themselves.

2.2 Research Design

The overall design was mainly exploratory and descriptive in nature. The research adopted both qualitative and quantitative approaches. Quantitative data aimed at generating information and explaining variables such as gender, social work employment, rural-urban dichotomies, positions occupied by social workers a educational approaches and levels of social work practice.

Qualitative analysis enabled a more insightful analysis of key variables that respondents were able to give elaborate explanations to. These included information on the different policies and programmes undertaken to tackle poverty, the progress made towards realization of MDGs (targeting especially constraints that can be addressed through social work's intervention), perceptions of roles of social work towards poverty reduction, and perceived strengths and gaps in the existing social work curricula, among others.

Quantitative methods

A survey was conducted with educators, students and practitioners. An interviewer administered questionnaire. A separate questionnaire with different sets of questions was designed for each target group.

Qualitative methods

Three methods were used to gather qualitative data. These are Key Informant Interviews, In-depth Interviews and Focus Group Discussions. The target groups were policy makers and clients.

2.3   Study Sites and Rationale for Site Selection

The study was conducted in four main provinces namely; Coast, Eastern, Nairobi, and the Rift Valley. The sites were selected on basis of the high number of social work education institutions, availability of practitioners, policy makers, educators, students and clients in the selected regions. Within each region, it was important to identify pockets of severe marginalization, poverty manifestation and other characteristics that were unique and important for selected regions. A national approach was critical in ensuring appropriate representativeness and coverage. Kenya comprises eight regions (previously provinces) that were used as a basis for sampling. Multi stage sampling design was therefore adopted, first selecting at least four regions. This was done through simple random sampling and the four regions selected were Nairobi, Coast, Eastern and Rift Valley Provinces.

2.4   Rationale for Selection of Target Groups

The study purposively targeted six categories of respondents. They were practitioners, employers, educators, students (Diploma/BSW), clients and key informants. Key Informants were policy makers in dockets of relevance to Social Work. Below is a brief description of rationale for each of the target groups.

(i)   Employers

Employers were informed about the roles that social workers play and the research project targeted organizations and/or agencies with social workers to obtain information on the engagement at organizational level of the impact, through the social workers, in reducing poverty and addressing MGDs. In order to have a representative set of employers from the various organizations that employ social workers in Kenya, it was important to ensure that lists of as many organizations as possible comprised the sampling frame. This was obtained through listing of these organizations according to international organizations such as the United Nations International Children's Emergency Fund (UNICEF), United Nations Development Program (UNDP), United Nations High Commission for Refugees (UNHCR), UN Women, followed by development oriented organizations such as Action Aid, World Vision, Plan International among others. The sampling frame of organizations with a scope for social work was generated from directories and complemented with the researchers' knowledge of their existence. This was listed and formulated along regional lines in order to ensure that all sampled regions were incorporated in the lists. Further engagement was sought within these organizations and the next stage for selection was purposefully done with employers who gave consensus for such research to go on within their organizations. The final tabulation in terms of the various organizations was in terms of whether they were public, private, private NGOs or private commercial. This classification was made by the employers themselves.

(ii)   Educators

Educators are at the core of not only assessing the roles played by social workers, but also contributing to the realization of MDGs. In this study, educators encompassed mainly social work lecturers within the universities that have social work training programmes in Kenya and all other identified social work training institutes in the country.

(ii) Policy makers

Policy makers are involved in creating an enabling environment in which social workers operate by enacting appropriate policies. If such policies prioritize and address poverty reduction it was envisaged that the impact of social workers will be greater. Policy makers were drawn from Government ministries, NGOs and international organization with a bias in social development interventions. Selection of these policy makers was on the basis of the likelihood that the targeted organization would have an input in policy making processes.

(iv) Clients

Clients are the direct recipients of social work interventions. They are useful in identifying gaps in the delivery of social work services. This group was purposively selected from the agencies that employed social work practitioners.

(v) Students

Social work students especially those who were in the final years in social work training institutes, colleges and universities were also included in the study. They were drawn from universities and colleges with accredited social work programmes.

All these categories of respondents ensured that the roles that social workers play are exhaustively discussed from different perspectives. The dynamics and challenges faced were also assessed. The various target groups from which data was collected is reflected in Table 1.

Table 1:   Distribution of respondents by study site

Study sites	Number of target groups					
	Practitioners	Employers	Educators	Students (Diploma/ BSW)	Clients	Key informants
Nairobi	50	20	10	5	2	4
Coast	50	20	10	5	2	3
Eastern	50	20	10	5	2	4
Rift Valley	52	20	10	5	2	4
Total	202	80	40	20	8	15
Grand total	365					

2.5   Description of Tools Used for Primary Data Collection

The main instruments used to collect primary data were:

2.5.1 Questionnaires

Four sets of questionnaires were used for the various categories of respondents namely social work educators, final year social work students, social work educators and social work practitioners. These tools contained both coded and open ended questions that sought to establish and seek correlations between social work education and practice, and the realities of how social work education informs and transforms the practice of social work. The tools were pre-tested within the four above mentioned respondent groups to endure the right interpretation and understanding of the questions asked.

2.5.2 Focused group discussions, and key informant interview schedules

Focus group discussions were conducted among clients with the objective of finding out their sectors in terms of engagement with different social work agencies in terms of services that they required and the extent to which the said services were provided. In addition, focus group discussions were conducted on the social work clients in order to assess their perceptions about those services and whether or not they had found them satisfactory. For the policy makers, who were key informants, the focus was to assess their level of engagement in formulating policies and strategies towards poverty reduction and realization of millennium development goals in Kenya.

2.6 Description of Secondary Sources of Data

Secondary data was used mainly to complement primary data. Sources of secondary data included National Development Plans, the Kenya Population and Housing Census 2009 (GoK, KNBS 2009) The First Annual Progress report on the Implementation of the First Medium Term Plan (2008-2010) and MDGs progress reports.

Table 2: Distribution of respondents by method of data collection and sample size

| Methods of data collection | Number of target groups | | | | | | |
	Practitioners	Employers	Educators	Students (Diploma/ BSW)	Clients	Policy Makers	Total
Survey	202	80	40	20	-		322
FGDs	-	-	-	-	8		8
Key informants	-	-	-	-		15	15

NB: Educators and students were drawn from the following institutions:

CUEA	–	Catholic University of Eastern Africa - Nairobi
Daystar	–	Daystar University - Nairobi
KISW	–	Kenya Institute of Social Work - Nairobi
UoN	–	University of Nairobi
GTI	–	Government Training Institute - Embu
SEUCO	–	South Eastern University College - Kitui
Kobujoi	–	Kobujoi Institute of Social Work and Social Development - Kapsabet
OTI	–	Other Social Work Training Institutions Registered with Ministry of Education

2.7 Quality Assurance in Data Management

2.7.1 Quality assurance

Quality assurance entails handling all the data that has been collected in a manner to ensure that the content and quality of data is well maintained throughout the research process (Agresti and Finlay, 1997). Before the data collection, research assistants were trained about accuracy in recording information from respondents both for qualitative and quantitative data. This enhanced the level of reliability for the research as standardized explanations were consistently interpreted by the whole team in the same way.

To ensure systematic handing of data, data storage and input was handled centrally. All questions as is the custom in research, were given identity codes which would facilitate the cross checking of data in case of any ambiguities during the data analysis process. Appropriate codes were maintained in the same format throughout data analysis which was conducted at this stage in time mainly to project frequencies of occurrence.

Qualitative data was preserved in its original format and only synthesized by key researchers as they made interpretations of the same data. Such data from the questionnaires, interview schedules, focused group discussions enriched the depth of analysis by giving insightful and detailed information about the issues being analyzed.

Quantitative data was managed by ensuring, before data collection, that questions were not miscoded. Further clarification was given as to how to respond to the coded questions, specifically one code answer only or multi-coded options. Where the questionnaire stipulated that only one answer will be accepted, then only that one code could be selected and this instruction was given in bold to ensure its adherence. For multiple response questions that allowed a selection of more than one code selection, then such a variable could have more than one code ticked.

2.7.2 Quantitative data analysis

Data was cleaned after collection to ensure a consistent and accurate data set. After obtaining the data sets, frequencies were ran to ensure patterns in variables were relevant and accurate as part of quality assurance before subjecting the data to analysis. Data was entered into the Statistical Package for Social Sciences (SPSS) for analysis of percentages and correlation between variables.

Missing data was recorded as missing data and not substituted for averages for quantitative data or general patterns for qualitative data. No methods of dealing with such missing data were applied. Any missing data out of the fact that the question was not applicable as a response from the respondent was coded 66 while that missing because the respondent did not answer the question was coded 99.

Some variables such as gender, educational qualifications, type of agency, levels of poverty that were either in nominal, ordinal or ratio format and appropriately coded as such allowed for cross tabulation analysis either in the form of cross tabulation tables or bivariate correlations (ratio or ordinal variables). Such connection between variables for example gender/age/educational qualifications and different aspects of social work helped in identifying objective patterns of engagement that were linked to the impact of social workers in the reduction of poverty and achievement of MDGs. Through SPSS, frequencies, graphs, tables extracted gave descriptive statistic measures useful in interpretation of the data. Such data made it possible to identify trends and patterns in the data.

2.7.3 Qualitative data analysis

Qualitative data analysis was done through consolidating responses and interpreting the answers according to trends and main themes along the topic of discourse. This was done manually after establishing key themes that were critical for the research finding. All questionnaires, interviews schedules and Focus Group Discussions content was read through and content analysis carried

14

out on the basis of identified main themes for discussion. Thus where in the above mentioned tools such information was evident, it was extracted as qualitative data that was the processed through content analysis.

A lot of qualitative data was generated from this study that gave insightful information and details about: social work practice, challenges faced by social workers, clients' interpretation of social worker's roles in poverty reduction, policy makers input on policy making and promotion of social work as a profession, the role of policy in addressing gender inequality and its effects in reducing gender induced poverty. Such data, obtained mainly from open ended questions, interview schedules and the Focus Group Discussions (FGDs) was important in clearly elaborating on roles played by different agencies in their support for social work and how that in turn influences the level of impact that social workers are likely to have in their service delivery.

2.7.4 Research clearance and other ethical issues

Clearance for the research was obtained from the Kenya National Council of Science and Technology (now the National Commission for Science, Technology and Innovation) to ensure that government authorities were informed and aware of the areas and targets to be covered in the process. Ethical issues such as confidentiality of the respondent, informed consent, accurate and objective data collection and reporting were adhered to in order to ensure that the whole research process would be credible, transparent and ethical.

2.7.5 Study limitations

Ideally, this study was relevant to all countries where high levels of poverty are reported. Such an assertion implies that the scope of addressing such a problem would be extended to all these countries many of them in Africa and Asia to enable appropriate intervention through social work practice and education. However this specific study focused on the Kenyan situation.

Whereas the study heavily relied on survey method in data collection, a more participatory methodology would have been ideal with respect to certain categories of respondents. This would have entailed, for example, observing social workers as they perform their roles and seeing the impact of their activities on their communities. Such an approach, however, was difficult given the various categories of the respondents and the time constraints of the project. From the triangulation of instruments, most of the key variables have been dealt with extensively and few gaps exist in terms of the information that would have been requested from the respondents. All in all the research project covered broad areas of issues well and in the future could be replicated in other regions of the world.

3

Poverty and Social Development in the Context of Millennium Development Goals

3.1 Introduction

The Millennium Development Goals (MDGs) is a blue print representation of global development as agreed upon by member states of the United Nations and development institutions (USAID, 2009). These goals are: Eradicate Extreme Poverty and Hunger, Achieve Universal Primary Education; Promote Gender equality and Empower Women; Reduce Child Mortality; Improve Maternal Health; Combat HIV/AIDS, Malaria and other Diseases; Ensure Environmental Sustainability; and Develop a Global Partnership for Development. The realization of these goals by the target date – 2015 is not easy due to several challenges revolving around the MDGs implementation process, stakeholders involved, country specific policies among others. Inadequate resources to facilitate the implementation of MDGs, skill acquisition for those involved in the implementation process and appropriate infrastructure for attainment of these goals remains a challenge in Kenya.

This chapter seeks to address two main tasks namely: an attempt to define poverty from multidimensional, contextual and complex perspectives and an analysis of the manifestation of poverty in Kenya and what is being done to address it with specific reference to the MDGs.

3.2 Defining Poverty

Defining poverty is difficult partly because of its relativity. In other words, poverty means different things to different people and in different places. In many African countries for instance, where the majority of people live in abject poverty, being poor is taken for granted. That notwithstanding, there are a spectrum of definitions. One of the most cited is by Sen (1985) who defined poverty as lack of capability to function in a given society. To him, poverty is about deprivation of ends. On his part, Horner (1994) noted that poverty is commonly associated with "a person who has few assets and no regular source of income, and who therefore struggles to meet his or her basic needs (and the needs of any dependants), would normally be considered to be poor. A locality, region or country with a large number of people living in such circumstances should in turn, also be regarded as poor".[1] In this definition, it is clear that poverty is associated with the level of material possessions, money and generally access to basic needs. It will vary from one country to another because of each country's unique circumstances, standards of living, cost of living and poverty lines.

Generally, poverty is associated with inadequate access to the basic necessities of life (food, shelter, clothing, health care and education), a feeling of powerlessness and helplessness; disenfranchisement; accentuated gender imbalance; isolation and social exclusion; erosion and loss of traditional cultures, values and social welfare systems; and inadequate capacity to utilize available resources.

Poverty can be relative or absolute. Absolute poverty means a standard of living defined in absolute terms using certain minimum level of subsistence as a benchmark. The problem with this standardized form of definition is that individuals and households present significant variations (Bellù and Liberati, 2005). The authors note further that relative poverty on the other hand varies depending on the different levels of standard of living enjoyed by individuals or households. Since the poverty line here is determined by the relative position of the rich, it would imply that relative poverty cannot be eradicated.

---

[1] Horner, Simon "Measuring Poverty" in the *Courier Magazine*, No.143 Jan – Feb.1994.

Within the broad definition of poverty, the poor perceive the problem differently from policy makers. According to the poor, poverty is: inability to have more than one meal a day, the increasing trend towards nuclearization of families, inability to cope with disease, not being on good talking terms with a neighbor, being disabled, landlessness, inadequate shelter, lack of household implements, loss of traditional skills and knowledge, lack of cash to buy clothing, lack of relatives to mention a few (Narayan, 2000). Local definitions therefore encompass social and personal dimensions of poverty, as well as material and non-material definitions of the phenomenon.

3.2.1 Social workers' definition of poverty

Among other objectives, the Promotion of Professional Social Work towards Social Development and Poverty Reduction in East Africa (PROSOWO) study, sought to establish how social workers define poverty. Out of the 202 social work practitioners interviewed, an overwhelming majority (85.1%) saw poverty simply as 'lack of basic needs'. To them, those living in poverty had no access to the following; decent shelter (e.g. living in slums), clothing, food and clean drinking water. Others (10.4%) noted that poverty was the 'inability to be self reliant'. Poverty here was seen as dependency or lack of self determination. The rest (4.5%) defined poverty either as a situation where one lives on 'one dollar a day' or where one thinks he/she is poor. The 'dollar a day' concept is the publicized World Bank delineation of the poverty line which could be misleading depending on the locality. For instance, one US dollar (about Ksh 85 at the time of the study) per person per day might be inadequate for subsistence in Nairobi but relatively adequate in a rural setting in Kenya. Table 3 shows the distribution of responses.

19

Table 3: **Per cent distribution of practitioners' definition of poverty**

Definition	Frequency	Per cent
Lack of basic needs	172	85.1
Inability to be self reliant	21	10.4
Living on less than a dollar a day	6	3.0
State of mind	3	1.5
Total	202	100

3.3.2 Manifestations of poverty in Kenya

Poverty in Kenya is attributed to a number of factors including: low levels of industrialization, misappropriation of public funds (corruption), low level of foreign investment, centralization of decision making, ignorance, environmental degradation, climatic change (e.g. drought and floods), poor planning and high population growth rates.

The manifestations of poverty include high levels of illiteracy, high infant mortality rates, poor housing, low access to safe water, crime, high levels of unemployment, rapidly growing informal settlements, poor infrastructure, hunger, and high prevalence of disease, low life expectancy, ethnic conflicts, child prostitution, child abuse and domestic violence.

The study sought to capture social work practitioners' experiences on social problems, and particularly poverty among their clients. Some of the problems cited include: poverty related issues (68.8%), child neglect (55.4%), food insecurity (26.2%), illiteracy (22.2%), and lack of school fees (15.8%) among others. Table 4 shows the whole range of responses.

Table 4:   Per cent distribution of major problems that clients presented

Major clients problems	Frequency	Per cent
Poverty related issues	139	68.8
Child neglect	112	55.4
Food insecurity	53	26.2
Illiteracy	45	22.2
Domestic violence	43	21.2
Poor health care	37	18.3
Lack of school fees	32	15.8
HIV/AIDS pandemic	25	12.3
Drug and substance abuse	16	7.9

From these responses, it is clear that all the problems identified are more or less poverty related. In fact, food insecurity, lack of school fees, poor health care and illiteracy are some of the most common manifestations of poverty in Kenya.

The social work practitioners were also asked about their impressions on the magnitude of poverty in their areas of operation. About 60 per cent were of the view that prevalence of poverty was 'high', 18.8 per cent felt it was actually 'very high' while only 3 per cent said poverty prevalence was 'low'. The distribution of the responses can be seen in Figure 1.

The distribution of the responses provides a glimpse of the needy socioeconomic environments in which social workers in Kenya operate.

Figure 1:   Per cent distribution of poverty estimates among the client population

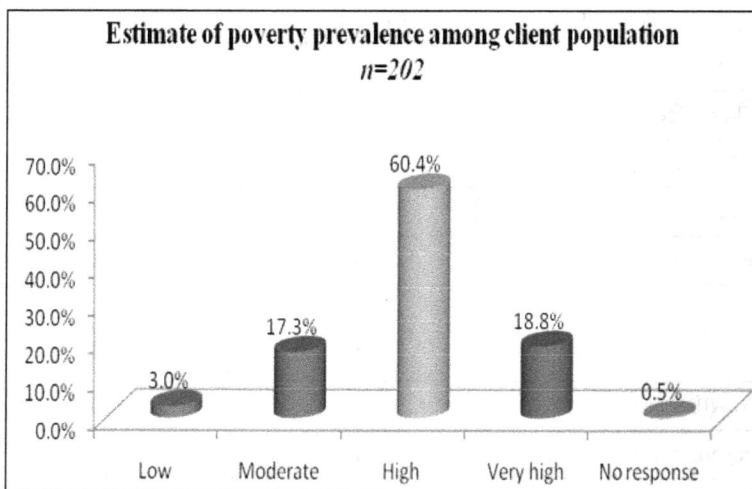

3.3   Programmes for Poverty Reduction in Kenya

Many African countries have been concerned with reducing poverty since they attained independence. However, poverty reduction has been an elusive goal, and most Africans are still among the poorest in the world to-date. Although Kenya, like most African countries registered substantive economic growth rates in the 1960's and early 1970's, there was a downturn from the 1980's. But even in Africa, there have been some success stories. The most unfortunate thing is that even with impressive economic growth rates, no particular country in Africa can claim to have won the war on poverty.

At Kenya's independence in 1963, the new Prime Minister then, Jomo Kenyatta, identified poverty, illiteracy and disease as Kenya's main development challenges. Unfortunately, those challenges remain the same almost 50 years later. Some measures though, have been taken in the effort to eradicate poverty in Kenya. These range from creating an enabling environment for investments and job creation, agricultural development and improvement of food security, water development and provision of education to improvements in health care.

While it can be assumed that nearly all government policies and plans are geared towards poverty reduction, some initiatives stand out. Key among these was the Special Rural Development Programme (SRDP) of 1970. In Kenya, like in many Sub-Saharan African countries, poverty eradication is almost synonymous with rural development as most of the population is concentrated in rural areas. In spite of the noble objective of enhancing food security and uplifting the general living conditions for the poor, the SRDP was abandoned in 1971, only one year after it was rolled out. Apparently, this was partly due to lack of support from the central government (Leys, 1975; Ergas, 1982).

Just over a decade later (1983), the government of Kenya crafted the District Focus for Rural Development (DFRD). Unlike the SRDP, the DFRD was better structured and more participatory. The district was to be the focal point in decision making, planning, resource allocation and implementation. But just like the SRDP, the central government played a very critical role in determining funding levels and supervision. Therefore, proposals made by communities were not honored. With time, it was clear that participation of the local people was extremely limited, and in many places, it was simply by name (Barkan and Chege, 1989; Chitere and Ireri, 2004). The DFRD had become inactive by the end of the 1990's.

Another initiative was the Youth Enterprise Development Fund (YEDF) mooted by the government in 2006 and launched in 2007. It was intended for the out-of-school, unemployed and marginalized youth so that they could be gainfully engaged through income generating activities. Under the fund, the youth were encouraged to join groups to get funding although individual enterprises are also supported. By September 2011, the fund had disbursed loans worth Ksh 5.2 billion to 144,000 youth enterprises (Fund Status Report,

2011). The YEDF however faces many challenges such as inadequate policy framework, defaulting on the loans, insufficient funds to cater for the demand, youth engaging in similar enterprises, lack of markets for the products and inadequate knowledge on business management.

The Women Enterprise Fund (WEF) was similarly launched in 2007. The aim was to empower women and their families. It had been noted that poverty in Kenya is gendered, with women being poorer than men. The fund, aimed at bridging this gap, was placed under the Ministry of Gender, Children and Social Development. Just like the YEDF, the WEF targets entrepreneurial women groups as well as individual enterprises. The WEF is underfunded, with only Ksh 1 million (USD 24,000) being allocated to each of the 210 electoral constituencies each year.[2] Although there are some success stories, many women have not been able to access the funds either due to non-availability or bureaucratic hurdles. Equal distribution of the money to the constituencies also ignores factors such as disproportionate distribution of the population and entrepreneurial culture.

Another notable development in the fight against poverty was the launch of Kenya Vision 2030 in 2008. This is basically a blueprint outlining a number of projects that should be implemented so that Kenya can overcome poverty and become a middle income economy by 2030. Key emphasis is provision of basic infrastructure, employment for poverty reduction, public resource management, Information and Communication Technology (ICT) and civil society and MDGs.[3] The first Medium Term Plan (2008–2012) of the Vision 2030 identified critical starting off projects. These included construction and fully equipping 560 secondary schools, having at least one boarding primary school in each constituency of the arid and semi-arid lands (ASAL) and recruiting 28,000 school teachers.

---

[2] Constituencies increased to 290 starting from 2013.
[3] The environmental cost of poverty to a society: The Kenyan experience by Mulongo Leonard; Kerre Patrick and Oseko Jacqueline. Source: www.weitz-center.org/uplo.

Other projections included to raise the primary to secondary transition rate to 75 per cent and the rate from secondary to university to 15 per cent. In the health care sector, the Medium Term Plan (MTP) proposed to have community level health units so that under-5-infant mortality rate could reduce from 120 to 33 per 1,000. There were also plans to increase deliveries by skilled personnel from 42 to 95 per cent and to increase proportion of immunized children below 1 year from 71 per cent to 95 per cent. In the housing sector, the plan set out to have 220,000 housing units build annually by 2012. This was partly to be done by providing incentives to the private sector to build houses. Individuals were to be supported through a 'secondary mortgage finance corporation'. Besides, Local Authorities would provide serviced land for low cost housing. As of now, it is not clear which of the targets set have been achieved.

It is also important to note that through the Ministry of Gender, Children and Social Development, there are cash transfer programmes for Orphaned and Vulnerable Children (OVC) and for the elderly (above 65 years) who have no alternative sources of income. In this initiative, care givers or those providing homecare to OVCs as well as the elderly and destitute receive Ksh 2,000 per month. The cash transfer programme is, however, beset by serious sustainability challenges as it is largely supported by development partners such as the Development for International Development (DFID) and United Nations International Children's Emergency Fund (UNICEF). Besides, due to the enormous numbers of those who require such support, the funds are grossly inadequate. In fact, among the elderly people, only 20 persons per constituency benefit from the cash transfer programme.

The Kenya Constitution (2010) has certain provisions that are critical in the war against poverty. First among these is the Bill of Rights, which guarantees every Kenyan access to education, food and medical care. The Bill of Rights also talks of affirmative action for minorities and marginalized groups, and freedom of movement, residence and from discrimination (one can therefore move and settle in any part of the country without fear of discrimination). Other notable provisions in the constitution include the creation of a devolved structure of government, in which the 47 counties will be allocated at least 15 per cent of total government revenue. Besides, there is an equalization fund for marginalized areas or with higher incidences of poverty so that they can be uplifted.

There are a couple of other new policies proposed to improve people's quality of life. These include the National Policy on Older Persons and Aging, the National Policy on Social Protection and the National Policy on Community Development. The government is also trying to implement a very controversial National Health Insurance Policy which has already stalled over corruption and structural issues.

3.4   Major Actors in Poverty Reduction

While it is easy to talk about the major actors in poverty reduction, it is a little bit more difficult to know which actor plays the greatest role. A look at the Kenyan scenario shows that each of these actors plays a very critical role in poverty reduction.

Multilateral and bilateral organizations supplement government effort particularly through general budgetary support. Each financial year, there is a percentage of the funding that is sourced from the development partners. In the 2011/2012 Financial Year for instance, this support amounted to Ksh 41.1 billion against a projected expenditure of Ksh 1.1 trillion. The support from development partners makes it possible to fund such pivotal programmes as the Free Primary Education (FPE), free day secondary education, free school feeding programmes (mainly in ASAL areas), school bursaries for vulnerable and poor households, water projects (drinking and irrigation), disease control (HIV/AIDS, malaria, immunization programmes, polio, etc), medical research, food relief during famines and support for the elderly persons. With regard to the specific roles played by social workers in poverty reduction effort

26

in the country, the study established that social workers had diverse interventions for different client groups including children, the elderly, families and other community groups. Some of the activities they were involved in included economic empowerment (54%), educational support (9.4%), training (7.4%) and provision of basic needs (6.4%) among others. Table 5 shows the spectrum of activities that social workers engaged to address the plight of the poor.

Table 5: Per cent distribution of social workers' roles in addressing poverty

Type of roles	Frequency	Per cent
Economic empowerment through IGAs	109	54
Educational support (clothing & books)	19	9.4
Capacity building through training	15	7.4
Provision of basic needs	13	6.4
Educational sponsorships	13	6.4
Cash transfers to OVCs and the elderly	10	5.0
Psychosocial support	8	4.0
Advocacy on human and child rights	6	3.0
Awareness creation to access health care	5	2.5
No response	4	2.0
Total	202	100

Most of the roles played by social workers in addressing poverty are child centered. Child specific programmes are seen as pivotal in the fight against poverty. Interventions such as educational support/sponsorships, OVC care and child rights among others are at the core of poverty reduction. To combat poverty, children should not only be targeted but actually involved. This is partly because they have the greatest potential to break intergenerational cycles of poverty. Children are Kenya's hope for transforming attitudes and behaviors about issues such as literacy, wealth creation, self

27

determination, gender equality and how people relate with the environment.

Second, it is encouraging to see that the largest numbers of social workers were actually involved in income generating activities (IGAs) or sustainable ventures such as educational support/ sponsorship. Only a few appeared to be involved in rehabilitative care (e.g. psychosocial support, awareness/advocacy). The majority of social workers equally felt that income generating activities were the most effective strategies in poverty reduction whether at the individual, group or community level.

It should, therefore, be noted that the role of social workers is eclectic embracing remedial, developmental and rehabilitative functions of social work.

3.5 Social Work and Social Development

When social work practitioners were asked to define social development, they noted that: it entails strategies geared towards poverty reduction; it is an approach that addresses socioeconomic aspects (basic needs, personal development, education, health and total well being); it is an all inclusive approach that cuts across all realms of social work interventions; and it is a societal based approach to development, among other things. Others associated social development with empowering individuals to have a better perception of the people and the environment around them, and investing in people to ensure improvement in their general welfare.

Social development means different things in different contexts. In human growth and development for instance, it may connote the qualitative changes in the transformation of human personality from childhood to adulthood (Grusec and Lytton, 1988). But it is also used in the context of socioeconomic development to show how societies grapple with social problems and promote community development. In this sense, social development has been contrasted with remedial or rehabilitative social work which has been the dominant mode of social work in many parts of the world. For some, social work is seen as synonymous with the remedial approach and therefore use social development to emphasize going beyond rehabilitation to equipping individuals, groups and communities with skills for self-reliance. In this sense, social development is associated with capacity building, empowerment, social advocacy, self-determination, community development, literacy and job creation.

Key issues that emerge from the foregoing discussion indicate that in spite of the fact that large sections of the Kenyan population still live in poverty, there are consistent efforts embarked upon since independence to improve the standards of living. It is also worth noting that social workers have been playing an important but often latent role in poverty reduction effort. Although social workers should be a visible driving force in poverty reduction, there are structural and historical factors that have made it difficult to achieve the goal. For instance, in nearly all the initiatives discussed above, social workers are hardly involved in the decision making process. That does not mean, however, that social workers are not involved in the actual poverty reduction initiatives. The evidence given above confirms this. Below is an attempt to link development programmes with the MDGs.

3.6   Programme Linkages to the MDGs

In the year 2000, world leaders agreed on the Millennium Development Goals, an ambitious agenda to promote sustainable human development in all countries. It turned out that six of the goals relate not only to children but also to poverty. They are: eradicate extreme poverty and hunger, achieve universal primary education, promote gender equality, reduce child mortality, improve maternal health, and combat HIV, malaria and other diseases. Special measures to protect the rights of the most marginalized communities are essential in achieving these goals.

It has been noted that MDGs have become the benchmarks to assess long term frameworks in national strategies and planning (Onyango and Schmidt, 2008). One of the goals of the PROSOWO study (2011) was to assess how social work practice is contributing to the realization or non-realization of the MDGs.

3.6.1 Social work practice and MDGs

The study revealed low levels of awareness of MDGs amongst social work practitioners. Out of 202 respondents, (5%) reported that they had never heard of MDGs. This was quite surprising as social workers are at the epicenter of MDGs realization. While the majority (56.4%) were aware of the MDGs, only 10.9 per cent knew about them 'in detail'. Besides, 27.2 per cent said they were 'slightly aware' of MDGs. This constituted a group of social workers who had merely heard of MDGs but did not know what they constituted and by extension, the social workers who do not link whatever they do with the realization of these goals. Figure 2 presents the breakdown of the responses.

Figure 2: **Per cent distribution of awareness of MDGs by social work practitioners**

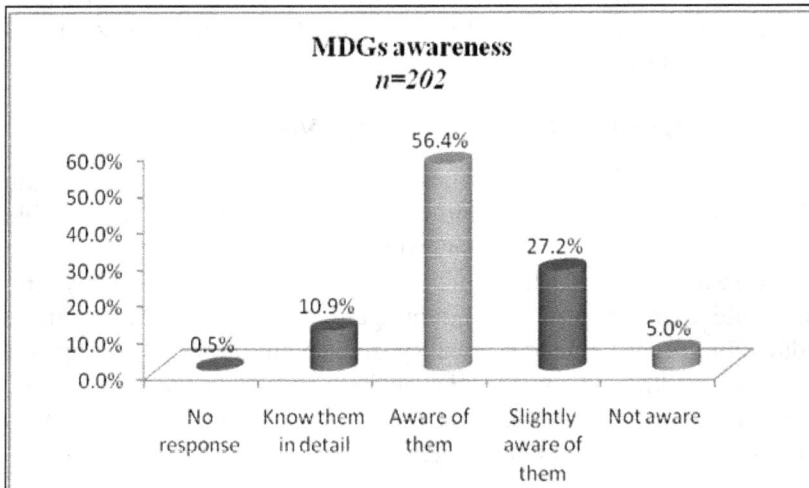

A similar pattern was noted among employers in relation to their awareness of MDGs. Out of the total number of 78 employers interviewed; only 53.8 per cent were aware of MDGs with only 19.2 per cent who knew about them 'in detail'. About 19 per cent were slightly aware of the MDGs while 7.7 per cent were not aware of MDGs. The 'slight' awareness or lack of awareness among employers to an extent mirrors the lack of awareness among social workers under their supervision.

Social work practitioners indicated that social work training does not adequately equip the trainees with requisite skills to address issues related to MDGs. Most of them (85.1%) reported that social work prepares one to adequately address issues related to MDGs but a few (14.9%) said that social work had not enhanced their competence to deal with MDG related issues. The variation in knowledge on MDGs can be as a result of factors related to the length of time a social work student spends in training (degree, diploma, certificate or 'on the job').

While the research team expected those pursuing social work at the time of the research (2011) to have some knowledge of MDGs, it was surprising to find that out of the 215 students that were interviewed, 5.6 per cent were totally unaware of MDGs while a whopping 25.6 per cent were only 'slightly aware' of the goals. In fact, only 14.4 per cent knew of the MDGs 'in detail' with 53 per cent were just 'aware' of the MDGs. Given that only 10.9 per cent of those in practice knew of MDGs 'in detail' it is somewhat imperative that those undergoing training today have a higher propensity to access information on MDGs than their counterparts who left college earlier. Figure 3 shows the range of responses from students.

31

Figure 3:   Per cent distribution of social work students' awareness of MDGs

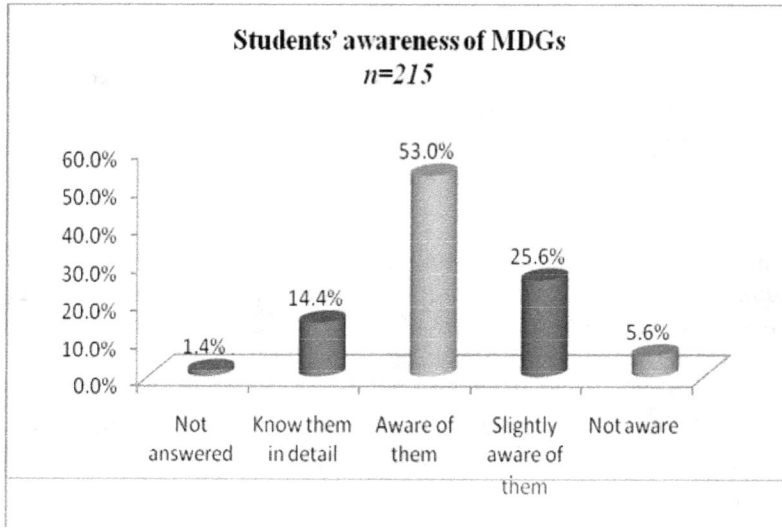

3.6.2 Programmes to realize MDGs

The study findings revealed that majority (83.7%) of social work practitioners were aware of the programmes undertaken in Kenya to realize MDGs. Some of these programmes identified include; Free Primary Education, promotion of health care services, gender equality, Kenya Vision 2030, youth and women enterprise funds, *kazi kwa vijana*[4] (work for the youth) and environmental conservation.

Majority of social work practitioners (67.3%) reported that the work they do contributes to poverty reduction and realization of MDGs while (22.7%) felt that their work contributed slightly to the

---

[4] *Kazi kwa Vijana* is a Kenya Youth Employment Project started in 2010 and intended to create temporary employment opportunities for young people particularly in the construction sites.

32

realization of MDGs. All the social work practitioners interviewed were engaged in activities that directly or indirectly contributed to poverty reduction. Table 6 indicates the distribution of social work practitioners who felt that they were making significant contributions to MDGs.

Table 6: **Per cent distribution of social workers making significant contribution towards MDGs**

MDG sector	Frequency	Per cent
Eradicate extreme poverty and hunger	136	67.3
Achieve universal primary education	140	69.3
Health (improve maternal health, reduce child mortality and combat HIV/AIDS, Malaria and other diseases)	116	57.4
Promote gender equality and empower women	99	49.0
Ensure environmental sustainability	62	30.7
Global partnership for development	154	76.2

As shown in the table above, social work practitioners appear to be making significant contribution to the realization of MDGs. There was no particular sector that was not receiving some attention. Many social work practitioners (76.2%) felt that they were in one way or another advancing the global partnership for development agenda. This was being done mainly in two ways, specifically forming networks with other local agencies while a few also had linkages with international organizations. Many social work practitioners were also advancing universal education mainly through provision of basic needs (such as clothing and food), sponsorships for school fees as well as vocational training. About 67 per cent indicated that they were involved in eradication of extreme poverty and hunger through programmes such as income generating activities and enhancing food production.

On health care, 57.4 per cent were involved in a range of health related activities namely improving maternal health, reducing child mortality and combating HIV/AIDs, malaria and other diseases. About 49 per cent were involved in gender empowerment through creating equal opportunities for women and also by building women's capacities. There is also a sizeable number of social workers (30.7%) engaged in environmental sustainability.

Social work practitioners and employers identified some initiatives that could be used to realize MDGs. These include: training to increase the social work practitioners knowledge on MDGs; creating awareness and empowering communities on the MDGs; incorporation of the MDGs in social work intervention strategies; networking with development agencies; promoting income generating activities (IGAs); promoting education; lobbying government for increased funding on poverty reduction initiatives; involving social work practitioners in policy formulation and implementation; and improving remuneration. Other suggestions were to mobilize community resources in order to reduce donor dependency, and developing strong monitoring and evaluation mechanisms.

Onyango and Schmidt (2008) argue that MDGs, though popularized as the guiding principles in national development, have a shortcoming. According to them, MDGs do not provide a comprehensive framework for strategic planning and action beyond the global targets. They suggest, therefore, that there is need for Kenya to set standards and thresholds. They argue that there is an assumption that the MDG targets are substitutable with nationally desired and allowable levels. This echoes an old concern in the developing world about adoption of proposals made by the industrialized world. Although some of these proposals may be made in good faith, implementation is often a challenge. To be fair to the so called Western powers, the hurdles encountered during implementation are often Kenya's own making. Combating of

HIV/AIDs is a case in point. Although Kenya was awarded USD 345 million in 2011 by the Global Fund to Fight AIDs, Malaria and Tuberculosis (*The East African*, 13th November 2011) and to assist in the war against those endemic diseases, that was the first successful application and approval of funding since 2008. Such funding has thus been infrequent and far spaced in between to have sustained impact. Finally, the suspension of the funding had a lot to do with unacceptable accounting procedures and suspected misappropriation of funds.

As Kenya awaits the evaluation of the Medium Term Plan (2008-2012) of Kenya Vision 2030, there are already concerns regarding whether the country is indeed on track to achieve the Millennium Development Goals. While the Free Primary Education was started in 2003 with a lot of fanfare and received international approval as an important milestone in the country's development, enrolments have since gone down, some schools have no basic facilities like classrooms and desks,[5] and many schools have inadequate number of teachers. The Government of Kenya is yet to recruit a total of 28,000 teachers as per the MTP, 2008–2012. These targets, however, are not being met because the country has no resources to meet the necessary costs but mainly because of other competing priorities.

Suffice it to say that as to whether Kenya will eventually achieve the Millennium Development Goals and Vision 2030, a lot depends on the extent of political will that will be expended in the process. Critical as well, is the role that social work practitioners can play to ensure that despite the challenges of the environment they operate in, they are able to use the resources and knowledge accrued to actually play a meaningful and effective role in the realization of Millennium Development Goals.

---

[5] In June 2012, a Citizen TV footage covering Kanduyi Constituency, Bungoma County, showed pupils learning in open air without classrooms and desks.

4

Dynamics of Social Work Practice in Kenya

4.1 Status of Social Work Practice

Social work is still a growing profession with very limited training institutions that are unable to meet the country's demand for social work professionals. Many social work training institutions have been unable to commence postgraduate programmes in social work owing to paucity of government funding among other factors. This in turn often frustrates many social workers, who silently quit the profession after undertaking post-graduate training in other non-social work fields (Lombard and Wairire, 2010). The consequence of the limited numbers of social workers in the country is that they have not been able to lobby strongly for a legislative Act of parliament that grants the profession recognition in line with other service professions like law or medicine.

Equally important to note is the fact that professional social work practice in the Kenyan context is largely generic. Specialized social work practice has not fully taken shape in Kenya probably because the profession is still growing and the need for intervention is quite overwhelming yet the general public is not fully aware about social work.

Specifically, the scope for social work includes but not limited to the broad areas presented in Table 7.

Table 7:   Summary of description of social work interventions

Types of social work interventions	Description of social work interventions
Community development	Interventions focus on small community groups e.g. women, youth, children, people with disabilities etc. Interventions depend on the needs of the said groups but are largely done at the community level through different programmes such as; adult literacy/awareness, income generation programmes through small micro finance services, health awareness programmes, environment up gradation, sites and service schemes in spontaneous settlements.
Child welfare services	Includes services such as: probation for child offenders, foster care including adoption, care for abandoned and rescued children, street children, orphaned and vulnerable children. Social protection is the primary social work role in these interventions.
Probation services	In this category, much of social work is practiced in the criminal Justice systems which include: the prison, the judiciary, correctional institutions for child offenders, juvenile courts, and community policing. Major functions served by social work here are largely rehabilitative, restorative and developmental with the overall aim of making the individual client get his rights even if convicted of breaking the law and/or be restored to fit in the society once again following the completion of his/her term in prison or custodial sentence.
Health care services	This often involves social workers in different health care settings playing different roles geared to enhance medicare provided by health personnel. Some crucial social work roles in this include social investigation to help the doctors fully understand patient conditions which may impact on treatment provided, patient/relative counseling, health education programmes, etc.

In all the areas highlighted above, the services provided cover both urban and rural areas. The mode of service delivery may vary depending on the agency, its focus and mandate and, the responsiveness of target beneficiaries to the services provided among other factors. In this study, majority of social workers were involved in direct service delivery in government and non-government organizations as seen in Table 8.

Table 8: **Per cent distribution of social work practitioners' views on their agency's main focus of intervention**

Focus of the organization's bulk work	Agency category				Frequency (n=202)	Cumulative per cent
	Government department (n=67)	NGO (n=110)	CBO (n=23)	Private (commercial) (n=2)		
Direct service delivery	21.3	34.7	5.0	1.0	125	61.9
Policy development	2.0	0.5	2.5	-	5	10.1
Advocacy	1.5	8.4	4.5	-	29	14.4
Social welfare administration	6.9	9.9	2.0	-	38	18.8
Others	1.0	0.5	-	-	2	1.0
No response	0.5	0.5	-	-	1	1.0

It should also be noted that there exists many other para-professionals i.e. people who are not trained in social work *per se* but who render social work services to different client groups on the basis of practice skills learnt through many years of practice by observing the trained social workers as they work in different settings.

4.2 Social Demographic Profile of Social Work Practitioners

4.2.1 Distribution of social work practitioners by sex

In the study, the distribution of social work practitioners was found to include 63.9 per cent female while 36.1 per cent were male. This is a reflection of the trends observable over the years in the enrollment of social work students at the University of Nairobi, the pioneer social work training institution at degree level in Kenya. A similar pattern appears in other institutions of higher learning where majority of social work students are female. Perhaps this could be as a result of historical feminization of social work and the assumption that women are more passionate on matters that affect human livelihoods and are socialized to be more responsive to social problems than men. The job designations that many get upon completing their studies at the university largely revolve around social work interventions with families, women and children and this explains why men tend to perceive social work profession as a domain for women.

4.2.2 Distribution of social work practitioners by age

Findings show that majority of social workers were below 30 years of age followed by those between 30–50 years as seen in Figure 4. It is encouraging to note that many social workers were devoted to the profession hence continued in the practice even after completing their training while still relatively young.

Figure 4: Age distribution of social workers

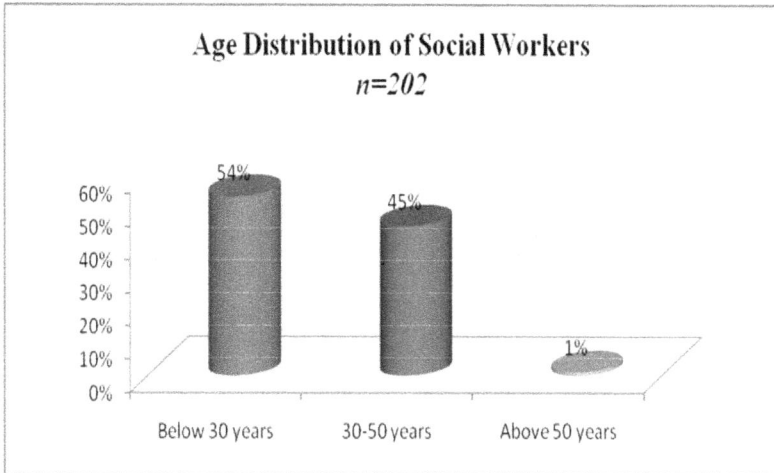

This is a reflection of the fact that given the right incentives, social work practitioners in Kenya can make lifetime careers in social work hence the need for more opportunities to advance their training for improved service delivery and commitment to the profession.

4.2.3 Distribution of social work practitioners by level of education

In the study, majority of social work practitioners' highest level of education was diploma qualification as shown in Figure 5. Perhaps this is due to the fact that there are more social work training institutions at the diploma level than those that offer training at degree level. In addition, diploma courses are also much cheaper and affordable.

41

Figure 5:   Highest education level of social workers

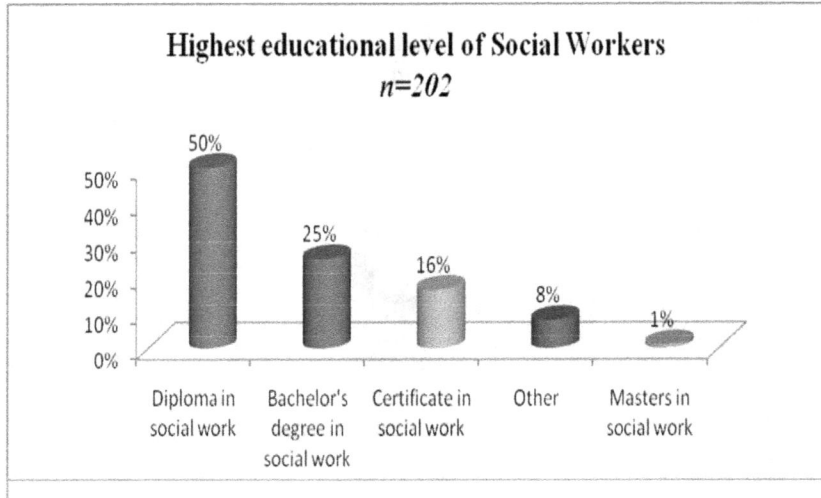

Notably, only 1 per cent of social work practitioners had a masters degree in social work as their highest education qualification. In addition, 25 per cent had a Bachelors degree in social work, 16 per cent had only a certificate while 8 per cent had other qualifications not related to social work. The findings reveal the need for more opportunities for social work training at higher levels. Perhaps it is time that employers of social work practitioners noted this and demand for higher qualifications which if done, may motivate the practitioners to aspire for the same. This however, cannot be realized in isolation of social work training institutions that must also make efforts to offer higher social work academic programmes with different social work specializations. Figure 6 further reflects that majority of social workers have had their training locally hence postgraduate programmes in social work can still attract many social work students at postgraduate level.

Figure 6: Institution where highest qualification was attained

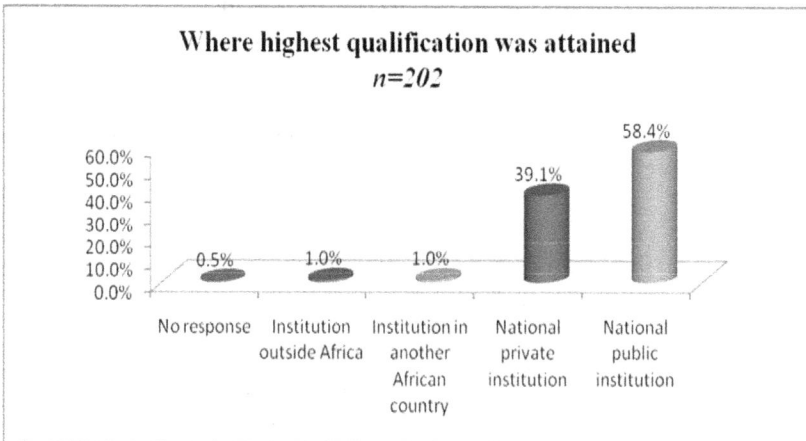

Where highest qualification was attained
n=202

58.4%

39.1%

60.0%
50.0%
40.0%
30.0%
20.0%
10.0%
0.0%

0.5%   1.0%   1.0%

No response | Institution outside Africa | Institution in another African country | National private institution | National public institution

4.2.4 Applied social work approaches

Although much of the training in social work is largely generic, the study found the practice to be largely developmental social work where 52 per cent of the respondents indicated it as the major focus of the bulk of work rendered by their employing agency. Majority of these respondents are in the Non-governmental Organizations (NGO) sector as indicated in Table 9. Developmental social work is defined as an integrated, holistic approach to social work that recognizes and responds to the interconnections between the person and the environment; links micro and macro practice; and utilizes strength-based and non-discriminatory models, approaches and interventions, and partnerships to promote social and economic inclusion and well-being (Patel and Hochfeld, 2008; Lombard, 2007; Patel, 2005; Mayadas and Elliott, 2001; Gray, 2006; Midgley, 1995 all in Lombard and Wairire, 2010). Mel Gray, (2006) opines that developmental social work affirms the commitment of the social work profession to social justice and human rights and to the eradication of poverty and inequality within a developmental social welfare system while Lombard (2007), clarifies that it positions the social worker as a role player and partner in social development in the social welfare sector

Table 9:   Per cent distribution of overall approach to service intervention by agency category

Overall approach to service intervention	Agency category					
	Government department (n=67)	NGO (n=110)	CBO (n=23)	Private (commercial) (n=2)	Frequency (n=202)	Cumulative per cent
Remedial/correctional/ therapeutic	13.9	13.4	2.5	-	60	29.7
Developmental social work	12.4	32.2	6.4	1	105	52
Generalist practice	6.4	8.9	2.5	-	36	17.8
No response	0.5	-	-	-	1	0.5

4.2.5 Applied social work methods

Although there exists a general feeling that the social work methods entailed in the social work curricula in Kenya are highly westernized, they still remain quite relevant in the Kenyan situation. Many social workers often find themselves using one or a combination of social work methods depending on the issue at hand and the nature of agency from where they render their services. In this study, majority of social workers were involved in individual case work across the three main agency categories namely government, non government organizations and community based organizations as indicated in Table 10.

Table 10: Per cent distribution of the type of social work method commonly used in interventions by agency category

Type of social work method	Agency category					
	Government department (n=67)	NGO (n=110)	CBO (n=23)	Private (commercial) (n=2)	Frequency (n=202)	Cumulative per cent
Individual case work	18.8	21.3	6.4	0.5	95	47.0
Group work	3.5	5.4	1.0	0.0	20	9.9
Community organization	2.0	11.9	0.5	0.5	30	14.9
Social development (broader/societal)	3.5	10.4	1.5	0.0	31	15.3
Social action	0.5	1.5	0.5	0.0	5	2.5
Social welfare administration	4.0	3.5	1.5	0.0	18	8.9
Social work research	0.5	0.5	0.0	0.0	2	1.0
No response	0.5	0.0	0.0	0.0	1	0.5

Much of individual social casework is practiced in the NGO sector. The data further indicates that social action and social work research are the least practiced methods of social work in Kenya at 2.5 per cent and 1 per cent respectively. This is probably because social action often involves radical intervention measures which may bring about conflict between the social worker and his/her agency or those targeted in order for the desired change to materialize. In addition, social action in Kenya has not been fully distinguished from mass action which is largely associated with violence and wanton destruction of property whenever put into exercise by those protesting or demanding to have some changes in place. This, however, may not necessarily be social workers but may include some civil society groups or political operatives and activists. Many, therefore, would rather not engage in anything likely to bring about open conflicts and hostilities between the social worker and the communities that are targets for the realization of desired changes and/or service.

4.3 Roles of Social Work in Poverty Reduction and Social Development

The role of social work in poverty reduction and social development cannot be underestimated. Key intervention activities undertaken by social work bring about change at individual, group and family levels. This change may be economic and/or psychological and sometimes affects all facets of an individual's life. The change often involves significant uplift in the status of an individual, family, group or even community, and sometimes helps in dealing with the trauma that is often associated with poverty. In all these, social work plays significant roles directly or indirectly. It builds the capacity and potential of individuals to understand and rediscover themselves, links them up with potential resources which can further consolidate the aspirations of individuals to meaningfully address the life challenges that confront them. It also builds up tangible skills to deal with such challenges, builds hope and empowers individuals singly or in groups to manage their lives with whatever resources they may have or facilitates them to acquire additional resources from external sources to address issues responsible for their poor state of life.

With specific reference to the roles that social workers play in the efforts to reduce poverty and thereby realize the Millennium Development Goals (MDGs), this study found that majority of social work practitioners played significant roles in equipping their client groups with relevant skills through empowerment strategies, community training and education and by direct activities with the potential to facilitate change as noticeable in Table 11. At the practice level, the respondents felt that to a great extent, social workers empowered their target population and also offered relevant training and education to practically help them out of the mire of poverty. The underlying implication here is that social workers impart relevant skills that would enable individuals to articulate themselves practically, train them on how to apply such skills and how to embrace the outcomes as they apply them in their daily lives. Such is the essence of empowerment which Ganayake and Ganayake (1988) postulate as:

> "a process that encompasses people in deciding where they are now, where they want to go, and developing and implementing plans to reach their goals based on self-reliance and sharing of power. Most importantly, it helps individuals and communities to liberate themselves from mental and physical dependence. It is in essence the ability to stand independently, think progressively, plan and implement changes systematically and accept the outcomes rationally".

Table 11: Roles played by social workers in poverty reduction and realization of MDGs

Per cent distribution of roles played by social workers in poverty reduction and realization of MDGs								
	Skill level				Practice level			
Role description	Not at all n=210	To a slight extent n=799	To a great extent n=1934	Not sure n=81	Not at all n=260	To a slight t extent n=855	To a great extent n=1810	Not sure n=98
Empowering target population	9.0	16.6	22.5	19.8	7.7	18.6	22.5	16.3
Educating /training target population	8.1	12.6	24.6	14.8	3.8	13.5	25.3	22.4
Facilitating change (change agent)	11.0	19.4	21.1	22.2	9.2	20.8	21.3	18.4
Brokering (linking to relevant resources)	19.0	21.9	19.3	21.0	13.8	21.4	20.2	20.4
Policy development	52.9	29.4	12.5	22.2	65.4	25.7	10.7	22.4

From the foregoing, therefore, poverty reduction strategies by social workers must not be limited to practical handouts alone but must also be backed up with relevant skills and adequate mental preparation hence the relevance of training and education for the target groups. It must comprise inputs that can strengthen the minds of the people, equip them with the desire and zeal to change, and at the same time strengthen their perceptions about the issues that they may need to change in their societal living.

Table 12: Socio-political issues that affect social development and poverty reduction

Issues	Frequency	Per cent
Political interference by politicians	47	27
Corruption	28	16.1
Lack of political goodwill	28	16.1
Poor leadership and governance	28	16.1
Tribalism	19	10.9
Influence of culture and traditional practices	11	6.3
Reluctance to change by community members	4	2.3
Ignorance of community members towards development projects	4	2.3
High dependency on leaders	3	1.7
Poor gender representation in politics	2	1.1
Total	174	100

The foregoing observations further suggest that poverty reduction strategies must begin in the mind where the target populations are first empowered and motivated to realize that they can change for the better; that their living conditions can improve and that they can overcome the dependency syndrome that often serves as a major obstacle to poverty reduction strategies. In addition, social workers must be alert to other social political factors that may negatively affect the efforts geared towards poverty reduction and social development. In the study, political interference by politicians, corruption, lack of political goodwill, poor leadership and governance were identified as the major factors that impact negatively on the efforts to reduce poverty and promote social development as noticeable in Table 12.

4.4 Professional Social Work and Realization of Millennium Development Goals

In the study, six important goals were prioritized with the specific goals of improving maternal health and combating HIV/AIDS, malaria and other diseases condensed as health. Majority of social work practitioners (76%) indicated that their organizations were more focused on the MDG goal - developing a global partnership for development. Achieving universal primary education (69%) and eradicating extreme poverty and hunger (67%) were the second, and the third rated MDG goals that social work agencies seemed to focus on respectively as indicated in Table 13. Gender equality and empowerment of women, and ensuring environmental sustainability seemed less prioritized by the agencies where social workers were employed.

It should nonetheless be noted that most agencies that employ social workers are not necessarily guided by MDGs in the process of determining what their specific areas of intervention would be but the vision and mission that they expound and which they tirelessly strive to realize. Equally important to note is the fact that there is no tangible evidence to the effect that social welfare agencies and other line ministries with a scope for social work align their intervention engagements with the UN Millennium Development Goals. Some goals however, may be addressed in the process but only as a by product of intended intervention focus.

Table 13: **Realization of Millennium Development Goals**

MDGs	Level of contribution	Frequency	Per cent
Eradicate extreme poverty and hunger	To a large extent	136	67.3
	Partly	46	22.8
Education	To a large extent	140	69.3
	Partly	30	14.9
	Not at all	32	15.8
Health	To a large extent	116	57.4
	Partly	46	22.8
	Not at all	40	19.8
Gender equality and empowerment of women	To a large extent	99	49.0
	Partly	57	28.2
	Not at all	46	22.8
Ensure environmental sustainability	To a large extent	62	30.7
	Partly	62	30.7
	Not at all	78	38.6
A global partnership for development	To a large extent	154	76.2
	Partly	15	7.4
	Not at all	33	16.3

A more in depth analysis of the MDGs prioritized by the social work practitioners complements the views above but went further to indicate the specific programmes that constitute the intervention activities undertaken by the organizations that employ those practitioners. As earlier noted, the MDG 'To establish a global partnership for development' was highly rated by the respondent practitioners. Further probe indicated that this was enhanced through establishment of linkages and networks with different development partners and/or agencies world over for concerted efforts to address issues for which the agency employing social workers exist. The building of linkages and networks was the main contribution at 79 per cent for realization of MDGs by the agencies that employ social workers as seen in Table 14.

Table 14: Specific MDG areas contributed to by social work agencies

MDGs	Specific area of organization's contribution	Count	Per cent
Eradicate extreme poverty and hunger	Reduce both poverty and hunger	116	57.4
	Reduce poverty	57	28.2
	Reduce hunger	9	4.5
	Not sure	20	9.9
	Total	**202**	**100**
Education	Sponsorships through bursaries	67	33.2
	Educational support (basic needs)	65	32.2
	Vocational training	30	14.9
	Adult education	7	3.5
	Life skills training	5	2.5
	Psychosocial support	4	2.0
	Peer education	2	1.0
	Not sure	22	10.9
	Total	**202**	**100**
Health	Combat HIV/AIDS, malaria, other diseases	100	49.5
	Reduce child mortality	51	25.2
	Improve maternal health	33	16.3
	Other health sector	18	8.9
	Total	**202**	**100**

MDGs	Specific area of organization's contribution	Count	Per cent
Gender equality and empowerment of women	Equal rights for all	93	46.0
	Build capacities for women	63	31.2
	Equal opportunities for women	28	13.9
	Not sure	18	8.9
	Total	**202**	**100**
Ensure environment sustainability	Protection of environmental & natural resources	65	32.2
	Improvement of sanitation facilities	50	24.8
	Improvement of drinking water	18	8.9
	Improvement of slums	15	7.4
	Not sure	54	26.7
	Total	**202**	**100**
A global partnership for development	Networks with other agencies	160	79.2
	Exposure to development initiatives outside country	8	4.0
	Not sure	34	16.8
	Total	**202**	**100**

A major possibility for this is the likelihood that the building of networks was central in linking social workers with different resource providers for their client groups at the family, group, individual and/or community levels. Moreover, there has been a notable reluctance by donor agencies to channelize their development funds through the government but through development agencies and civil society groups, faith based organizations and community based organizations. A network of such agencies was, therefore, vital for global partnership for development.

Achievement of Universal Primary Education was the second rated MDG that different social work agencies were contributing to. A major factor for this is probably due to the overwhelming response by donor agencies to support the Free Primary Education Programme spearheaded by the National Rainbow Coalition (NARC) government between 2003-2008 and the Grand National Coalition government between 2008–2013. Much of this support was in the form of school bursaries, provision of basic needs for school going children e.g. school uniform, books, a mid day meal in areas struck by extreme poverty levels, etc. This support was also noticeable for orphaned and vulnerable children and others who needed vocational training upon completion of elementary education as indicated in Table 14.

Eradication of Extreme Poverty and Hunger was yet another MDG goal highly rated, and with several intervention activities in place. To a certain extent, this goal appears to be the most significant and one that cuts across all others. A poor person is usually hungry, and often unable to access even the basic healthcare, hence making him vulnerable to frequent illnesses. Poverty and illiteracy or poor education often go together, and in addition, further exposes the victim to other vulnerabilities including low self esteem. Breaking the cycle of poverty on the other hand is not easy hence perpetuating the trauma of poverty in affected individual, families and communities.

It is for this reason that several social work agencies engaged significant measures to fight poverty such as: community empowerment, community training, and civic education for appropriate skills to improve livelihoods, educational sponsorship for needy children, etc. Table 14 further highlights other MDGs significant areas that social work agencies contributed to with specific reference to each stated Millennium Development Goal.

4.5 Challenges Facing the Social Work Profession

Professional practice of social work in Kenya has for a long not been easy owing to a wide range of factors. These range from the very basic preparations social work students undergo at the training level, the kind of exposure they get during field education, the work environment in which they operate in employment, the collegial relationships that determine their professional duties among others. In a nutshell therefore, it can rightly be argued that the challenges that confront social work as a profession are mainly centered on training, work environment and the practitioners themselves.

With regard to challenges associated with training, the major problem is the lack of social work trained personnel with a sound social work knowledge base for the different levels of social work training. Majority of social work educators in Kenya are holders of undergraduate degrees in social work. This is largely attributed to the fact that at the time of this study, no institution of higher learning in Kenya was offering post graduate training programmes in social work. However, post graduate training in other related areas such as sociology, psychology, religion and/or other social science disciplines is offered. The Catholic University of Eastern Africa started the Master of Arts in Social Work shortly after the study was done. The lack of social work educators trained at higher levels may therefore explain why Kenya does not have diverse specialized training programmes for social work personnel. This further contributes to the sustenance of traditional social work courses yet social change and emerging technologies are constantly yielding new social work dimensions that require change in social work curriculum.

Nonetheless, the social work training in place cannot be dismissed in terms of preparing social work practitioners for different tasks and obligations in their pursuit to assist their client groups improve their social functioning and livelihoods in general. In this study, social work training was found to have sufficiently (57%) prepared the practitioners to work in diverse cultural settings within which different client groups experience different problems and issues as indicated in Figure 7.

Figure 7: Social work training for adverse cultural settings

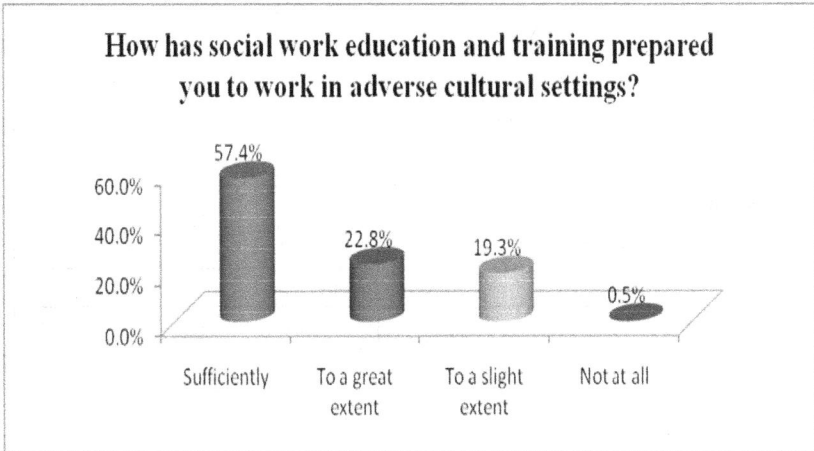

However, a critical look at the training level still yields more challenges for the social work trainee, and may in future be a challenge in actual practice. The hands on field practicum cannot be said to be sufficient enough to offer the trainees adequate exposure for social work practice in adverse situations since most training institutions are in urban areas and most trainees do their field work in the same areas. This, coupled with other factors in the practitioner's social environment often brings about additional challenges such as retrogressive traditional beliefs and practices, cultural conflicts with agency programmes particularly where the intended beneficiaries of the social worker's initiatives chose to stand by their cultural orientations rather than adapt to the changes pursued by social work practitioners. Table 15 reflects some of the challenges that confront social workers in the course of their practice. Most of them are largely influenced by the work environment in which the

55

practitioners operate in while others are a reflection of multiple issues that pose challenges to social workers in their practice.

Table 15:   Common challenges faced by practitioners related to culture and traditions of the clientele

Practitioner dilemma and challenges	Frequency	Cumulative per cent
Cultural conflicts with agency programmes	64	36.8
Retrogressive traditional beliefs and practices	37	21.3
Gender discrimination issues	15	8.6
Child custodial issues	14	8
FGM	10	5.7
Marital conflicts	9	5.2
Language barrier	9	5.2
Age differences between social workers and clients	5	2.9
Witchcraft issues	3	1.7
Handling HIV/AIDS victims	2	1.1
GBV	2	1.1
Inheritance and succession issues	2	1.1
Drug abuse	1	0.6
Property ownership	1	0.6
Total	**174**	**100**

Besides the challenges specified in Table 15, others are caused by factors far beyond the control of social workers and are largely policy related. Key in this is the lack of adequate resources to support and/or complement social workers at different points of interventions. The area coverage for social workers may sometimes be overwhelming yet they have very limited resources in terms of human resource, money and materials. This is not withstanding the dwindling number of trained social workers hence the practitioners in the field often experience burnout as a result of having to deal with more cases than they could possibly handle. The main policy related challenge is closely linked with the lack of legislative mechanisms, for example an act of parliament for strong professional body of social workers with a clear mandate to regulate itself and the other service delivery process for social work clientele. These and other related challenges are highlighted in Table 16.

Table 16: Other factors that confront social workers in their practice

Other factors given by social work practitioners	Frequency	Cumulative per cent
Inadequate resources to support social workers	128	44
Inadequate professional social workers	57	19.6
Poor policy planning and implementation	26	8.9
Lack of a professional body to regulate social work practice	25	8.6
Lack of government support in social work projects	11	3.8
Lack of knowledge on MDGs	9	3.1
Lack of appreciation of social work profession	8	2.7
Corruption by stakeholders	7	2.4
Cultural conflicts with agency programs	5	1.7
Lack of adequate training materials	4	1.4
Lack of community participation in development issues	4	1.4
Lack of harmonized curriculum in both public and private institutions	4	1.4
Harsh environmental conditions for social workers	3	1.0
Total	**291**	**100**

4.6   Professional Identity of Social Workers in Kenya

A major challenge for social workers in Kenya hinges on professional identity. This again is as a result of other factors, which from a critical perspective are not entirely beyond the practitioners. Professional identity is greatly determined by the existence of a vibrant professional body that is holistic in representation and clearly visible with a sustained membership, and clearly defined roles to ensure that practitioners own it and feel part and parcel of such an organization and its activities. Regular and sustained forums through which professional colleagues engage each other, and where feelings of comradeship are generated and sustained together with clear articles of association are some crucial aspects for professional identity of social work practitioners.

Unfortunately, this has not been the case in Kenya. Asked if they were aware of any social work association in the country, 68 per cent of social work practitioners indicated they were not while 32 per cent stated they were. Asked if they were members of a national social work association in Kenya, 97 per cent of the respondents indicated they were not while a paltry 3 per cent indicated they were members. This is a pointer to the fact that the existing association must rejuvenate itself by inculcating the facts above for more visibility and sustained activities geared towards bringing social workers together for a united voice and impact in the country. It is important to note that most respondents (95%) felt that if given a chance, they would join an association for professional social workers while only 4 per cent felt otherwise. This, therefore, indicates that all is not lost; practitioners are ready and willing to join hands as professional colleagues through a legally established association that is visible, with a clear mandate to speak for social workers and with well established structures and mutually agreed guidelines for effective management of such a body.

Besides this, there is a general feeling in Kenya that social work as a profession has not yet attained public recognition and that many underestimate it. One may clearly see this right from the time university students come to enroll for the bachelor's degree in social work at university level. Majority of students at such a point in time rarely know anything about social work and often confess they had never heard about it before. Some learn about social work from their seniors at the university while others get to know about it through other sources such as NGO's. Unlike other professional courses such as medicine, engineering, law, education etc in which students undergo a competitive process to gain admission, such is not evident in social work probably because the profession is not fully known in terms of content, scope and social work personnel. This, therefore, explains why social work intake is usually low for many universities in the country.

On the other hand, the entry level in the civil service for social workers is usually not on par with that of other civil servants. Social workers have been employed at a grade lower than their contemporaries e.g. probation workers, children officers, labor officers, personnel officers etc. For this reason, many opt to be employed simply as children officers than under the label 'social workers' for faster progression in career ladder. Other cadres with no requisite social work qualifications are often employed for the very same jobs that are meant for social workers which in turn directly or indirectly demotivate the morale of social workers in public service and ultimately goes on to affect their professional identity.

The study established that over half of social work practitioners (54%) felt that social work has not yet gained public recognition and that it was highly underestimated as indicated in Figure 8. In the instances where social work is adequately recognized or highly appreciated, chances are that the social work practitioners are employed by NGO's or parastatal organizations that recognize the professional inputs of social work in their service delivery. Such organizations, therefore, pay the practitioners well and engage them regularly in diverse roles.

**Figure 8:   Social workers' views about public recognition of social work
profession**

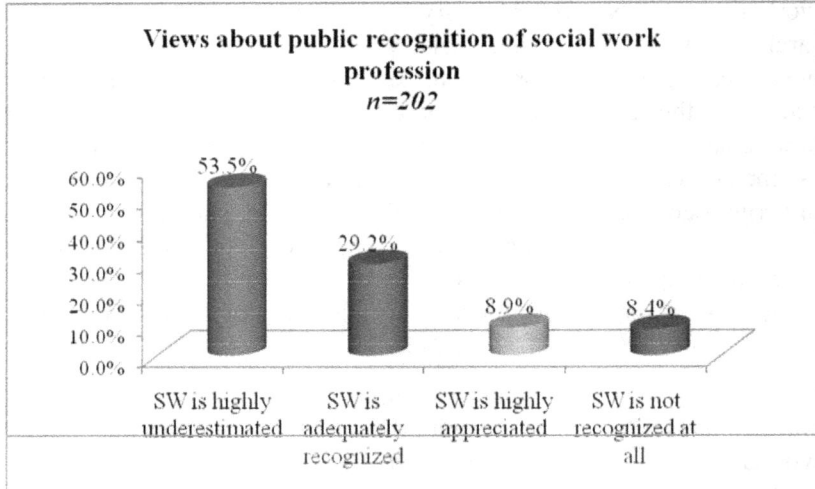

Views about public recognition of social work
profession
n=202

4.7   Repositioning the Place of Social Workers as Agents of Change

From the foregoing, a lot more needs to be done to reposition the current situation of social work practice and in the process improve the professional identity of social work and thereby redeem its status in society. Several stakeholders and actors must play their roles unreservedly for this to materialize. This includes the academics and respective institutions of higher learning, the social work trainees and practitioners themselves, social work employing agencies and the government as well. These stakeholders must engage positively with a clear focus to strengthen the social work profession and to generate a positive public image of the profession that is sustainable in all spheres within which social workers operate.

At the training level, institutions of higher learning must aggressively promote professional social work education by marketing social work programmes that they offer and by establishing cordial relations with agencies that accord their students field education opportunities. Sustained exchange of social work knowledge between social work academics and the personnel who supervise social work students during their field practicum will go a long way in consolidating the role of social work in the service delivery process of those agencies. Perhaps a once in a while field work seminars between the social work academics and field agency supervisors held at the institutions of higher learning will on the other hand accord the agency fieldwork supervisors a feel of social work in the learning institution and thereby complement the congenial efforts of boosting professional social work identity. This will further ensure that both practitioners and academics get a better forum to exchange ideas particularly on new emerging issues in social work theory and practice.

For the social work trainee still undergoing social work education at university level, tangible efforts that inculcate a sense of support and commitment to social work profession must be explored and impacted in the learners. Strong service values and work ethics that resonate well with social work profession must be implanted in the learners while still in college in order for them to visualize the profession with commitment and internalized pride for serving the society as social workers. This is likely to lift up the spirit of social workers whenever they undergo adversities in the course of serving their client groups in future.

The government on its part must hasten the process for relevant legislative structures to ensure that social work profession is fully legislated with appropriate legal acts in place. These will further strengthen the profession by regulating its core duties, requirements for practice including essential training and a conducive work environment for social workers. This is in addition to requisite salary that does not degrade the dignity, self worth and moral of social work practitioners amidst existing harsh economic realities that often confront them every now and then.

5

Reflections on Social Work Education and Training

5.1 Introduction

The unique role that social workers play in the prevention, management and resolution of social problems has impacted on the development goals of many countries (Abbot, 2002; Banks, 2001; Ife, 2002). This has been facilitated by the expansion of social work education and training initiatives which have grown exponentially in the last twenty years, notably, in the pacific region, Eastern Europe and Africa. Social work education focuses on humanitarian and democratic ideals, values of respect, equality, worth and dignity of all people (Lundi, 2006).

Social work practice has focused on meeting human needs and developing human potential (Healy and Link, 2012). Human rights and social justice serve as the motivation and justification for social work action (Ife, 2002). In solidarity with those who are disadvantaged, the profession strives to alleviate poverty and to liberate vulnerable and oppressed people in order to promote social inclusion. Social work values are embodied in the profession's national and international code of ethics.

Macro social work suggests that the purposeful design of interventions that target organizations is relevant to communities (Rothman, 1996; Weil, 1996; Kettner and McMurty, 1993). However, the accurate intervention is a function of the prevailing circumstances for, example, in Zimbabwe the profession has been seriously undermined by the negative political and economic situation of that country (Mupedziswa and Ushamba, 1999).

The acquisition of skills and knowledge is influenced by the understanding of social work as a profession. In recent years the internationally accepted definitions of social work, that...

> ... social work as a profession promotes social change, problem-solving in human relationships and the empowerment and liberation of people to enhance well-being...

has come under scrutiny. A revised and updated definition by the International Federation of Social Workers (IFSW) and the International Association of Schools of Social Work (IASSW) states that social work is:

> ... a practice-based profession; an academic discipline that promotes social change and development, social cohesion; and the empowerment and liberation of people... (IASSW, 2004)

has improved the understanding of social work. As Hoefer (2006) notes, social work focus will encourage practitioners across the globe to expand their vision of the profession in a more holistic way, and in terms of the complexities of people interacting with their environment. This in turn, will influence the shaping of the curriculum in terms of relevance to social work education outputs that target a particular society.

Social work is a value based profession that operates within a dynamic environment. There is need, therefore, for constant re-evaluation of the contextual paradigm against which the skills are acquired. At independence, Kenya which is ranked as a low income country, embarked on a development agenda that was meant to ensure that the three enemies of development: poverty, lack of education, and diseases would be removed. Fifty years later, despite various initiatives that have been put in place, including sessional papers on development, *kazi kwa vijana*[6] initiatives, more recently

---

[6] An initiative for youth through funds centrally disbursed from the government. Other initiatives include such funds to women and entrepreneurs in the small and medium sectors

the Kenya Vision 2030, realization of the MGDs, and the Constitution, many Kenyans still live in abject poverty with all its challenges including educational, occupational and health inequalities.

As Rothion (1999) observes, there is need for specific interventions to deal with the factors that hinder the maximum actualization of the well being of individuals in their respective situations. Social workers have provided such interventions through working with done in communities. For social workers to be effective in their practice, they must receive adequate and relevant education to enhance their role in reducing poverty and meeting the targets of the MDGs.

Social work education and training is crucial in this endeavor. Information from practitioners, educators, employers and clients derived through the PROSOWO study made significant contribution in assessing the level of engagement between social work education and training and its impact on the practice.

This chapter, therefore, reflects on social work education and training in Kenya and discusses the two issues with a view to assessing the extent to which social work education contributes to the reduction of poverty, and the realization of the MDGs. It also aims at exploring additional challenges encountered in social work training provides some highlights on how to best enhance the practice.

5.2 Policy and Legal Environment for Social Work Education and Practice

The policy and legal environment influences social work education and practice. In the Kenyan context however, there is no direct legal and policy framework for social work education and practice because social work is yet to gain legal status as a profession duly recognized and backed with corresponding state statutes. Nonetheless, various social welfare policies and development blue prints have shaped the development agenda, on which social work programmes should hinge upon. After independence, the Sessional Paper No.10 of 1965 on African socialism laid the basic foundation for working with self help groups in the process of dealing with the problems of living that affected individuals and communities and, as a means for planned development in Kenya. The Constitution has also been a guide for development in the country and this document which was recently revamped is taking into consideration issues of inequality which are a cross cutting theme for social work. The Kenya Vision 2030, is founded on three important pillars namely: social, political and economic, and also has significant scope for social work, and more particularly in the framework of the social pillar which focuses on building a just and cohesive society, that enjoys equitable social development.

Social policy and its reconstruction, has significant social implications in terms of casework, group work and community work. It also has implications in the approaches that are used in social work. The 10th World Social Work Conference in Rome in 1960, emphasized the importance of influencing social policy, policy development and social planning in order to target key issues in communities that would be better addressed through such policies. Where such policy is supported by a legal framework, it gives the basis for the enactment of that policy. This is mainly because what the policy advocates has been anchored in the legal framework and thus the issue of implementation is addressed. Finally, this helps to create a better framework for the practice and also for social work education.

In the PROSOWO study, the level of participation by social work educators in Kenya's policy development and social planning was low with 5.3 per cent, not participating at all, 52.6 per cent participating to a small extent, 36.8 per cent to a moderate extent and only 5.3 per cent reported that they participated to a large extent. This is a very small percentage, suggesting that important issues at policy making level may be leaving out the educators who are at the core of identifying critical issues that may inform policy and legal framework in the teaching and training of social work. Such issues include as increased social exclusion, unemployment, poverty, multicultural issues and integration policies. Changes the in social policy framework imply changes in professional standards and responsibility, in establishing vocational standards and skills, competence and professional development, integration of knowledge skills and values.

5.3 Social Work Training Curriculum in Different Institutions

The development of standards for the education and training of the social work profession by the International Association of Schools of Social Work (IASSW), and the International Federation of Social Workers (IFSW) generated controversy from its inception (IASSW, 2004). The debates centered on four issues that in the long run impact on how training in social work is imparted. The debates were around issues of globalization or localization, dominance of western or the global North's conceptualization of social work over indigenous practice models, multiculturalism or universal values, and the global standards or local standards (Gray and Fook, 2004).

Standards for the core curricula are reflective of specific societies and countries where the curriculum is inculcated into social work education material. This has several considerations that need to be met including the domain of the social work profession. For each specific region, there is the need for social workers to focus on key areas to address and what need to be understood and internalized. For example, issues of poverty and gender inequality are more prominent in developing countries relative to the developed ones. There is also need to understand knowledge of human behavior and development, within the context of traditions, culture, beliefs, religion and customs.

In 2000, the board of IASSW commissioned a world census of social work programs and established a permanent standards committee charged with tracking programme development as part of IASSW commitment to social work education (Barretta-Herman, 2005; Garber, 2000). The data in the membership survey was descriptive and demographic, with a focus on programme structure, international activities and the curriculum.

5.4 Perceptions of Social Work Practitioners About the Adequacy of Social Work Training

In the IASSW study, educators were asked to prioritize the courses that their students undertook at Bachelors or Masters level. Popular courses listed included social work theory and methods, ethics and values of social work, social policy administration, community development, history of social work, human growth and development, race, ethnic and cultural issues, organizational theory, social environment, social planning, sociological theory, law and economic theory. This research did not ask either educators or students to indicate the courses covered in the curriculum of their various learning institutions but rather focused on the curriculum in terms of the underlying approach either generalist, social development, traditional remedial/therapeutic, community development and social policy planning and administration. Other components and measurements of the concept are discussed in subsequent sections where issues of the curriculum are discussed.

The challenge of social work education in Kenya is to produce a professional with the ability to get involved, empower the client, apply the right to confidentiality and privacy and instill loyalty in clients. Moreover, such a professional should be able to meet the challenges at an institutional level which include the need to develop networks across institutional boundaries and develop good working culture while at the same time engaging citizens in an active and meaningful way.

One way to assess the impact of social work education is through an analysis of the perception of the practitioners in terms of their assessment of how that education has contributed to their professional practice as social workers. An understanding of the background training of these practitioners is therefore critical. The majority constituting 50 per cent of social workers are trained at diploma level, 16.3 per cent at certificate level, leaving only 33.7 per cent with bachelors and postgraduate qualifications. Of these, 24.8 per cent have undergraduate degrees specifically in social work, and 7.9 per cent who are social work practitioners have degrees in related fields such as sociology, community development, development studies, project planning and management, law, psychology, community health and development, and counseling psychology. The one per cent representation of those with Masters degrees and PhD degrees is an indication that most of them are likely to be educationists.

The training of social work practitioners is bottom heavy and one takes into consideration the level and content of social work advancement across educational levels, nearly two thirds of social work practitioners do not possess knowledge and expertise at degree level and above, where there is more rigor in the theoretical and practical training of social work.

Most of the training (58.4%) has taken place at national public institutions, 39.1 per cent at national private institutions with less than 3 per cent having been trained in Africa or outside Africa suggesting little influence from outside the country and the likelihood of a standardized national approach in imparting social work education. National institutions lead in the awarding of the highest proportion of bachelor's degrees, followed by national private institutions and last institutions from outside Kenya as indicated in Figure 9.

Figure 9:   Awarding institutions and highest levels of qualifications

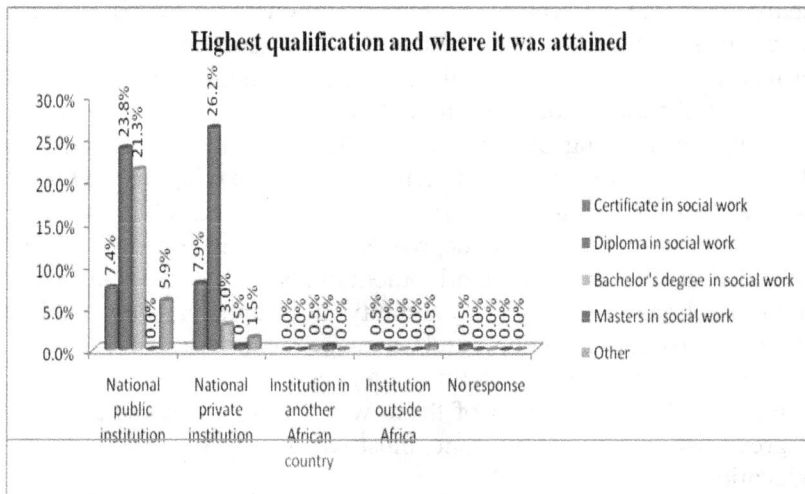

Practitioners holding degree qualification obtain them mainly from national public institutions, who to a lesser extent also have qualified diploma and certificate holders. On the other hand, national private institutions have qualified social workers across board at certificate, diploma and masters level. In fact, none of the practitioners with masters qualification had obtained it from a national public institution. But also surprisingly, very few bachelors qualifications have been obtained from national private institutions. National public institutions lead in the allocation of bachelor's degrees in social work while national private institutions are favored by practitioners for master's degrees but that is not the case for bachelor's degrees suggesting either the lack of such programmes at major public universities or minimal enrollment for such programmes in national private institutions. This in turn raises fundamental concern that the capacity for training of social work has not been tapped into and the gap in the advanced training of social workers translate to a large proportion seeking training in institutions outside the country.

On whether social work practitioners in Kenya are ably trained to deal with the diverse and complex nature of the profession, the findings indicated that Kenyan social work practitioners had various responsibilities ranging from field work, home visits and office work. Most of the work that social workers engaged in was mainly making changes in client's lives for long term improvement in their socioeconomic status (55.4%), followed by addressing the immediate needs of clients (34.7%), and preventing clients from falling into undesirable situations (9.9%). Most of the practitioners therefore dealt with immediate situations rather than long term and preventive measures.

In making interventions for long term improvements, social work practitioners interacted with clients experiencing high levels of poverty which was indicated as a key problem encountered by 98.5 per cent of the practitioners. Interacting with poverty related problems was therefore eminent among Kenyan social workers as they served clients in the community. The sectors served or included development (27.7%), education (25.2%), health (17.3%), gender (5.9%), food security (1.5%) and other (22.3%) sectors of their agency's focus. Few social work practitioners were involved in gender and food security sectors, probably suggesting that inequalities in these fields still need attention and refocusing.

Given this background, practitioners rated social work education in the context of how it was presently assisting them in various components of their work, specifically in addressing diverse social problems, the issue of poverty as a social problem, preparing them to meet local communities and helping them to integrate gender issues in social work interventions as indicated in Table 17.

Table 17: Impact of social work education on aspects of social work practice

Aspects of social work practice	Impact of social work education										
	Not at all		Very little		Little		Much		Very much		Frequency	Cumulative per cent
	n	%	n	%	n	%	n	%	n	%	n	%
Social work education and training has helped address diverse social problems	1	0.5	3	1.5	32	15.8	61	30.2	105	52.0	202	100
Poverty was adequately covered in social work/education	9	4.5	14	6.9	33	16.3	73	36.1	73	36.1	202	100
Training helped to work and relate to local communities and their conditions	2	1.0	6	3.0	21	10.4	58	28.7	115	56.9	202	100
Training helped to appreciate and integrate gender issues	2	1.0	6	3.0	26	12.9	61	30.2	107	53.0	202	100

A slight majority (52%) asserted that the social work education training that they had received was relevant for addressing diverse social problems. 82.2 per cent connected their ability to deal with social problems to the social work education that they had received. 83.5 per cent indicated that the social work they had received had an impact in leading them to appreciate and integrate gender issues while 85.6 per cent indicate that their social work education had helped them to relate to local communities and their conditions. The findings suggest a linking at a high level of social work education and thee roles played by social workers.

Nevertheless, when it comes to the coverage of poverty in the social work curriculum (72.2%) suggests a gap in the way poverty is handled and thus a low level of preparedness in dealing with poverty related issues. Thus a total of 14.4 to 27.7 per cent of the practitioners indicated that social work had not at all or had prepared them a little suggesting the need to interrogate the reasons for this.

From the perspective of the practitioners, the following challenges in social work education and training are inherent: lack of adequate social work educators (18.9%), lack of recognition of social work profession (14.6%), more theory than practice in the curriculum (11.8%), lack of revised curriculum to handle current social issues (10.2%), lack of adequate training materials (10.2%), lack of accredited social work training institutions (8.7%), few social work training institutions (7.5%), lack of a professional social work body (5.5%), high cost of social work training fees (4.3), lack of employment opportunities for social workers (3.1%), lack of proper coordination between training institutions and agencies (2.4%), lack of harmonized curriculum between private and public institutions (1.2%), lack of social work masters programme, lack of government support in social work progammes all with less than one per cent. The reasons for the outcomes of not feeling adequately prepared give a nexus for the factors that need to be further scrutinized to ensure that they are remedied.

Practitioners also experience various cultural and political issues while practicing, significant of these being teenage marriages (14.4%), male chauvinism (13.3%), traditional beliefs and cultural differences (11%), female genital mutilation (10.3%), gender discrimination issues (9.1%), witchcraft (8,4%), religious differences between Muslims and Christians, child custodial issues, language barriers, marital issues, inheritance issues, resistance to the abandonment of retrogressive beliefs and practices, widow inheritance, gender based violence, incest, polygamy, religious and cultural holidays, child naming, tribalism, HIV/AIDS, circumcision (boys and girls), and child labor among others. Only 22.8 per cent are prepared to a great extent by social work education to deal with these diverse social and cultural settings, with 19.8 per cent feeling completely unprepared and 57.4 per cent only sufficiently prepared.

Understanding and being able to interact with culturally and politically diverse settings is crucial for social work and thus more emphasis needs to be put into social work education in this area. Only 12.9 per cent of practitioners felt that the current models of social work practice compatible with the cultural values and traditions in their areas of operation, with 21.3 per cent reporting little or no compatibility leaving 65.8 per cent asserting compatibility between the current models of social work practice and cultural values and traditions. The overall professional ability to deliver culturally sensitive and appropriate social work practice was rated as very highly by 6.4 per cent of the practitioners, highly by 58.4 per cent, moderately by 32.2 and low at 3 per cent. Thus, if we consider those who ranked themselves at highly and very highly, 64.8 per cent were confident in their professional ability to deliver culturally sensitive and appropriate social work practice while a significant percentage (35.2%), were not.

Cultural capacity of the practitioner implies that social workers must have cultural competence if they are to work successfully. The language and skills that social workers bring to their community practice will play an important role in ultimately determining their roles and the likelihood of success.

5.5 Perceptions of Educators About the Social Work Curriculum

At the 2009 world conference on higher education, the United Nations Educational, Scientific and Cultural organization (UNESCO) recognized the important role of higher education in preparing students for their work in the global era (Healy and Link, 2012).

Faced with global challenges, higher education has the responsibility to advance the understanding of multifaceted issues which involve social, economic, scientific and cultural dimensions and the ability to respond to them. In order to move towards this purpose, higher education institutions must be actively engaged in the world around them through partnerships, providing a global perspective in the direction they provide and connecting the local and the global. For the case of social work, internalizing the curriculum will allow social work educators to transcend parochialism, understand similarities and differences among nations and prepare students for emancipatory practice (Sewpaul, 2001).

In focusing on shared problems, the International Association of Schools of Social Work asked participating schools in Africa to seek for strengths and innovations from county to country to help find solutions to cross border challenges such as AIDS, child soldiers and poverty. Social work education is increasingly responding to these calls for recognition of the international and global responsibilities of higher education but more work remains. Educators also need to play a role in the preparation of social policy and programs for social work educational programmes which must ensure that professionals are prepared with requisite knowledge and skills and attitudes for practice.

Developing new curriculum for social work programs and modifying existing priorities in the light of the vision and mission of social work educational institutions departments is key. The global standard for the education and training of social work state that each social work educational institution should develop a specification of its programme objectives and expected higher education outcomes (IASSW, 2004). These programme objectives should indicate how the programme addresses local, national and/or regional/international development needs and priorities. Educators must also bridge social work theories and practice. It is therefore against these standards that the social work curriculum can be evaluated.

From the sample of 19 educators from various institutions that train social workers in Kenya, 63.3 per cent were from private commercial institutions, 26.3 per cent from public/government owned institutions and 10.5 per cent from private-NGO/religious institutions. It is worth noting that, social work programmes in Kenya started as early as 1964, spearheaded by the Government Training Institute, and thus most of these institutions have had enough time to evolve and review their curriculum overtime *vis a vis* the challenges of development over time.

The specific areas interrogated about the curriculum include how social development is taught within the institutions and the relevance of social work curriculum to the development needs of Kenya and in the realization of the MGDs. Educators' own level of education is probably an indicator of the adequacy of social work education delivery. Barretta-Herman (2005) notes that that the level of PhDs in social work is limited, is an MSW in social work. From the information from educators, those with bachelors degree constituted 31.6 per cent and masters 15.8 per cent. There were few PhDs in the sample data. This is consistent with other trends especially in the developing world, where the main challenge is to address the impediments and gaps facing some of the renowned public universities that do not have a PhD programme in social work. This was further supported by the fact that 21 per cent of social work qualifications were obtained in Europe and Asia. For those who obtain their qualifications locally, 68.4 per cent were from national public institutions, 15.8 per cent from national private institutions, 5.3 per cent from within Africa and 10.5 per cent from outside Africa.

The underlying approach in the current social work curriculum was described by educators as mainly: generalist (52.6%), community development approach (36.8%), social development (5.3%) and social planning and administration (5.3%). The curriculum probably leans on a generalist approach and community development. This is where the emphasis is placed *vis a vis* social development and social planning and administration. Social development is taught mainly as a cross cutting approach throughout the curriculum (42.1%) and; as a separate module (31.6%) and as a course unit in given subjects rather than it getting an emphasis of its own, yet social development links directly with development issues and concerns. The non specific approach that this unit is given may explain the delinking between the skills acquired and demands of practice.

The data suggests low levels of aligning the curriculum to the global standard of social work education and training, little emphasis on social development and more emphasis on generalist and community development approach which may create a weak link in the skills taught to social work students in order to address poverty issues. A general issue also emanates from a gap in re-training as social workers may not be upgrading their skills after the initial bachelors and as they practice. The environmental changes imply a need to upgrade skills in masters where the data shows very few social work students are enrolled.

Majority of educators (68.4%), indicated that global standards of social work education were only partly integrated in the curriculum at their institutions of learning. 5.3 per cent were not aware of the global standards while 26.3 per cent asserted that such global standards are fully met in their curriculum. This suggests the need to have the global standards for social work education actualized within the indigenization discourse.

Curriculum reviews were a facet of many institutions with 73.7 per cent having reviewed their curriculum within the last 5 years and suggesting a constant review of the curriculum. However, 26.3 per cent had not done so. The quality of the review, the frequency of the review, the relevant changes of the review that make the curriculum more focused in helping to tackle poverty reduction and achieving of

MDGs needs to be factored into the discussion to ensure that the curriculum review process is actually targeted and in line with actualization Kenya's development goals. The context for curriculum reviews is usually an assessment of whether a review of the curriculum has been done or not. In this study, a chi square (3.13, 2df) at alpha 0.05 depicted no relationship between the institution undergoing curriculum reviews and with the curriculum meeting the global standards suggesting that the lack of meeting of the global standards may be a result of other factors, and not necessarily a review of the curriculum, even though the sample size was small.

Nevertheless, there is generally high level of acceptance from educators that the social work curriculum is relevant to the development needs of the country and specifically the attainment of MDGs (84.2%). The rest (15.8%) of the educators did not perceive such a link. This suggests that nearly one in every four to five educators did not perceive that the curriculum was directly linked to the achievement of MGDs; this is relatively high, but this information is important as it suggests that more mechanisms to enhance causal links needs to be put in place to actualize the effective relevance of the curriculum towards the attainment of MDGs. The right mechanisms have to be put in place by planners in education to ensure a connection between the actual content and the attainment of MDGs.

Research is a critical aspect of learning within social work practice. Its outcomes have the potential to inform the major areas in the social work education curriculum that require to be revised consistently in order for social work trainees to adequately respond to different issues of social work concern in their practice and work environments. From the findings, 63.2 per cent asserted that they conduct research in social work. A fairly large percentage (36.8%) did not conduct research in social work and development issues. This creates a gap in the empirical testing of theory and vice versa. It is suggested that this proportion is also not in touch with the current social work issues that are emerging from research, and that they are not imparting the relevant skills for a crucial component in social work. Such research skills enable social workers to learn the skills of assessment and link various key variables of explaining phenomena accurately, something they do even as they practice.

At least one in every five social worker educators did not conduct research themselves, bringing into focus the potential lack of current skills that are practiced through research by educators. The majority, (52.6%) conducted research to a moderate extent and 26.3 per cent to a high extent that is determined mainly from emerging social issues (26.3%), through other researches (26.3%), from consultations with other stakeholders (10.5%) and individual interests (5.3%). Surprisingly the non response on this aspect was very high (26.3%) which may suggest that the level of research is not as high as presented.

The engagement of social work educators in policy development and social planning was low with 57.9 per cent minimally engaged, 36.8 per cent engaged to a moderate extent and only 5.3 per cent engaged to a large extent. Where there is an engagement in policy development and social planning, it is mainly through workshops (36.8%), policy stakeholder debates and consultancies (31.6%), advocacy in various institutions and agencies (10.5%) and through research on social work issues (10.5%). Educators gauged the effectiveness of the curriculum through various indicators shown in Table 18.

Table 18: Educators' assessment of skills and competencies of social work graduates

Social work skills	Assessment of skills and competencies											Frequency	Cumulative per cent
	Strongly disagree		Disagree		Not sure		Agree		Strongly agree				
	n	%	n	%	n	%	n	%	n	%		n	%
Curriculum explicitly refers to national poverty reduction and development strategies	1	5.3	1	5.3	-	-	10	52.6	7	36.8		19	100
Graduates are adequately equipped to address issues of poverty	1	5.3	4	21.1	1	5.3	7	36.8	6	31.6		19	100
Graduates have adequate skills and competences in integrating social and economic development goals	-	-	1	5.3	-	-	15	78.	3	15.8		19	100
Curriculum prepares graduate for the achievement of UN MDGs	-	-	-	-	1	5.3	12	63.2	6	31.6		19	100

Social work skills	Strongly disagree n	Strongly disagree %	Disagree n	Disagree %	Not sure n	Not sure %	Agree n	Agree %	Strongly agree n	Strongly agree %	Frequency n	Cumulative per cent %
Assessment of skills and competencies												
Graduates play a role in protection and promotion of individual rights	-	-	-	-	1	5.3	10	52.6	8	42.1	19	100
Knowledge and skills in gender issues at all levels of practice	-	-	3	15.8	3	15.8	7	36.8	6	31.6	19	100
Theories and models enables students to work in adverse cultural settings	-	-	1	5.3	1	5.3	11	57.9	6	31.6	19	100
Knowledge and skills to handle challenges and needs of rural areas	-	-	2	10.5	1	5.3	10	52.6	6	31.6	19	100
Collaborations with other schools for the exchange of staff, students and literature	2	10.5	4	21.1	1	5.3	8	42.1	4	21.1	19	100

Overall trends indicate that educators generally agree that graduates attain skills and competencies for social work practice at varying levels across the indicators. The higher percentage of agreement was that graduates have adequate skills and competencies in integrating social and economic development goals, while the least percentage agreed on the extent of institutional involvement in academic discourses, and collaborations with other schools. However, at higher levels of making these assessments, where educators strongly agree across the indicators, the percentages are smaller across all indicators with more confidence exhibited among educators that graduates play a role in the protection and promotion of individual rights. Adding up 'agree' and 'strongly agree 'indicates that educators' best assessment to least assessment, thus moving towards the bottom of this list indicated below is indicative of areas where educators assessed the more wanting skills of the graduates. The findings indicate that the areas of concern that educators feel have not been adequately addressed are those at the bottom of the list below. Thus for example, collaborations with other schools is an area more wanting than knowledge of gender issues in all levels of practice.

1. Graduates play a role in protection and promotion of individual rights.

2. Curriculum prepares graduate to achievement of UN MDGs.

3. Graduates have adequate skills and competences in integrating social and economic development goals.

4. Curriculum explicitly refers to national poverty reduction and development strategies.

5. Knowledge and skills to handle challenges and needs of rural areas.

6. Theories and models enable students to work in adverse cultural settings

7. Graduates are adequately equipped to address issues of poverty.

8. Knowledge and skills in gender issues in all levels of practice.

9. Collaborations with other schools for the exchange of staff, students and literature.

From the educators' rankings, lower assessments are inherent in the gaps in knowledge and lack of specification of information to aid social work practice in rural areas, inadequacy in dealing with culturally specific settings, not having skills to address poverty, gender issues and gaps in collaborations among institutions.

5.6 Experiences and Perceptions of Students about the Social Work Curriculum

Most of the students were females (71.2%) while males accounted for only 28.8 per cent of the respondents. The majority (54.4%) of these students were in public government learning institutions, followed by 34.9 per cent in private commercial institutions and 10.7%) in private either NGO or religious affiliated institutions. Nearly 50 per cent (48.8%) were to graduate with a diploma in social work, another 46.5 per cent with bachelors degree in social work and 4.7 per cent with certificate in social work. Further analysis was disaggregated along the level of educational attainment *vis a vis* the students' perception about the social work curriculum.

Table 19: Students' perceptions about the focus of social work programs

Focus of social work programmes	Frequency	Cumulative per cent
Clinical/therapeutic social work	5	2.3
Community development	71	33.0
Social welfare administration	18	8.4
Generalist social work	90	41.9
Social development	25	11.6
Not sure	3	1.4
Not applicable	2	0.9
Not answered	1	0.5
Total	215	100

Most students perceived the bulk of social work programmes as mainly generalist (41.9%), followed by community development (33%). The conceptualization of students and those of practitioners about the general approach to social work concurs in terms of a generalist and partly community development approach. Table 19 indicates the findings.

In terms of research as an important aspect of the curriculum, 86.5 per cent of the students undertook research while 13.5 per cent did not. This is a fairly large percentage of those who did not take research training. A cross-tabulation analysis indicates that these are mainly diploma students and there is a statistically significant relationship between the social work programme and propensity to undertake research work as shown in Table 20.

Table 20: Social work programme and undertaking of research

Social work programme about to graduate in:	Do you undertake research course/unit as part of social work curriculum?		
	Yes	No	Total
Certificate in social work	8	2	10
Diploma in social work	83	22	105
Bachelor's degree in social work	95	5	100
Total	186	29	215
Chi square = 11.55, 2 df, statistically significant at .003 levels of significance (please note that one cell is less than 5)			

In terms of the orientation of research problems, these mainly they tilt towards community development (44.7%) and problems specific to vulnerable groups (27.4%). The students gauged the level of attained social work education competencies as indicated in Table 21.

Table 21: Students' assessment of social work education competencies

Social work skills	Assessment of social work education competencies													
	Strongly disagree		Disagree		Not sure		Agree		Strongly agree		Not answered		Frequency	Cumulative per cent
	n	%	n	%	n	%	n	%	n	%	n	%	n	%
Issues of poverty and poverty reduction adequately covered	4	1.9	20	9.3	5	2.3	135	62.8	50	23.3	1	0.5	215	100
Knowledge and skills in social and economic development goals	3	1.4	3	1.4	6	2.8	118	54.9	85	39.5	-	-	215	100
Social work training acquired in MDGs awareness	2	0.9	24	11.2	17	7.9	113	52.8	58	27.1	-	-	214	100
Realization of MDGs	3	1.4	12	5.6	17	7.9	114	53.0	68	31.6	1	0.5	215	100
Protection and promotion of individual and social rights	1	0.5	6	2.8	8	3.7	103	47.9	95	44.2	2	0.9	215	100
Gender issues in curriculum	3	1.4	4	1.9	1	0.5	105	48.8	102	47.4	-	-	215	100
Gender issues in all level of practice	1	0.5	8	3.7	7	3.3	119	55.3	79	36.7	1	0.5	215	100

Social work skills	Assessment of social work education competencies																
	Strongly disagree		Disagree		Not sure		Agree		Strongly agree		Not answered		Frequency		Cumulative per cent	
	n	%	n	%	n	%	n	%	n	%	n	%	n	%		%
Addressing local problems and needs	2	0.9	5	2.3	10	4.7	78	36.3	120	55.8	-	-	215			100
Work in diverse cultural settings	2	0.9	1	0.5	6	2.8	69	32.1	137	63.7	-	-	215			100
Remedial/therapeutic/individual social work methods	2	0.9	12	5.6	15	7.0	123	57.2	63	29.3	-	-	215			100
Development issues such as poverty reduction	1	0.5	10	4.7	9	4.2	119	55.3	76	35.3	-	-	215			100
Deeper understanding of development needs in community	4	1.9	11	5.1	9	4.2	82	38.1	107	49.8	2	0.9	215			100
Knowledge and skills to address individual problems	4	1.9	3	1.4	5	2.3	87	40.5	114	53.0	2	0.9	215			100

Students assessed themselves very highly at being able to work in diverse settings (63.7%), addressing local problems and needs (55.8%), and having knowledge and skills to address individual problems (53%), areas across which educators had expressed concerns were not ranked highly. Across all indicators, apart from addressing local problems, working in diverse cultural settings and knowledge and skills to address individual problems, students tend to agree rather than strongly agreeing that they possess the relevant skills; indicating gaps in the perception by students that their acquisition of the skills is not upto standard. Across significant indicators, there are substantial proportions of students who altogether strongly disagree, disagree and are not sure of skill acquisition among the given variables, the highest percentage of these combined responses being: not having skills for creating awareness about MDGs (20%) followed by lack of social work skills in remedial/therapeutic/ individual social work methods (13.5%).

5.7 Field Practice Education as Part of the Social Work Curriculum

Fieldwork is part and parcel of the curriculum, as indicated by (94.7%) of respondents, compared to only 5.3 per cent of responses from educators who indicated that field practice is not engaged in the curriculum, albeit this response was mainly from private non-commercial institutions. Field practice is structured into the curriculum as a separate unit and supervised by lecturers (92.7%) and also as a mandatory assignment given to students during a specified period (5.3%). There is a bias in fieldwork placements in urban areas thus student miss opportunities for rural settings dynamics and training. The findings indicated that fieldwork placements, where over 70 per cent should be placed in rural areas, are representation is very low, at only 10 and 5 per cent. This means that overall there is very low rural fieldwork placements.

Most of the placements are done directly through placement of students to agencies by the training institutions (50%), students making their own arrangement (30%), through recommendation and introduction letters (10%). The biggest consideration for proceeding for field work is that a student should have adequately covered the basic social work foundation courses in the curriculum (32.1%) and that specific areas of specialization are taken into consideration as adequately covered (21.4%), the interest of the student (17.9%), proximity of students' residence to agency (10.7 per cent), and relevance of the agency to social work. These high rates for taking up field placements confirmed by the social work practitioners of 89.6 per cent whom had undertaken field work placements while studying social work. The higher number of placement was between not more than two (77.2%) and between 3 and 5 placements (10.4%). Most institutions have at least two mandatory field practicums. The number of field placements was particularly higher for students who undertook social work training during the early years of the 1990's when the 8-4-4 system of education was implemented at university level.

As per the projected pattern from educators, rural field practice is limited with 53.5 per cent of practitioners having no rural field practice experience, while those having up to two field work placements being date account for 44.1 per cent. Those who have up to two field placements representation from practitioners are accounted for at 54.5 per cent, and the non response rate is at 42.6 per cent. Many of the agencies where practitioners worked offer internships to social work students (80.2%), in 54.5 per cent of the cases the practitioner is involved in supervision while nearly in 45.5 per cent of the cases, there is no involvement of the social work practitioner in supervision. This has serious implications for the training of social workers. Supervision is necessary as it provide the critical avenue for correction and positive readjustments. Due to lack of such supervision the implication is that the fieldwork experience has not been enriched.

Practitioners were asked generally for an indication of fieldwork areas that need improvement within academic institutions. According to the respondents, the areas that need to be addressed include proper advance fieldwork planning (25.7%), increasing the field work period (19.8%), completion of the syllabus before field work (18.3%) and proper supervision by lecturers (15.3%). They suggested that receiving agencies should actively involve students in community projects (32.7%), provide proper field work supervision by agency staff (13.9%), and motivating the students through stipends (11.9%). Students, their indicate that major fieldwork areas for improvement include adhering to professional social work ethics (44.1%), actively involving students in community projects (10.9%), willingness to learn new ideas (10.4%), and specialized field areas of interest (7.4%).

From the students' perspective, field work is considered as part of the training (89.9%) with only 9.8 per cent stating that they did not undertake field work. With regard to the nature of services and social work methods, most of the field work placements are within community organization settings (55.3%), remedial/individualized services (13%) and group work (13%), only 7 per cent was done in the advocacy services. Again the bulk of field work placements reflect the concentration in community service and development.

According to educators, the most common type of agency for field work placements was NGOs (59.5%) followed by government departments (23.3%) and CBOs (10.2%). 65.1 per cent of the field work placement was done in urban areas *vis a vis* 28.4 per cent in the rural areas.

5.8   Indigenization of Social Work Education and Training

The components of social work education are broad. Weaver (2006), identifies the following areas: ethics and values of the profession, that social work is a mission to help disenfranchised people, that the inherent dignity and worth of the person must be maintained, client self determination/informed consent, importance of social environment. In the indigenization debate, these components are assessed and understood from an indigenous perspective to make them acquire a specific meaning within a specific context.

Sometimes there are gaps between social work implementation and the needs and desires of the indigenous people. Where the context of the needs and desires of the people is not taken into consideration, intervention may not be well targeted to solving the problem as even that may not have been well conceptualized. It has also been argued that an over emphasize on professionalism may distance social workers from indigenous people. This may also happen when social workers serve as agents of social control. Sometimes social workers are perceived as naïve and uneducated about indigenous peoples and as clinicians with little focus on advocacy or social justice. The indigenization debate within an African context is informed and reflected by the fact that social work is informed not only by specific practice environments and Western theories, but also by indigenous knowledge. For indigenization to be fully applied all these issues must be adequately addressed.

In terms of the indigenization of social work, 84.2 per cent of educators asserted that they contribute to the discussion of indigenization of social work in Africa. Only 15.8 per cent did not participate in such discussion. However it is worrying that even though these educators might have been contributing to the indigenization debate, that in itself may not be indicative of the level of application in content materials and lectures. This realization is made more evident by the responses that educators gave regarding challenges in the indigenization process. Educators pointed out the following challenges with regard to indigenization the process: lack of adequate teaching materials (26.3%), lack of adequate resource materials (21.1%), lack of support from stakeholders (21.1%), diverse African cultures (15.8%), ideological conflicts (10,5%) and lack of experience on the issues (5.3%). There was a very high use not usage of materials produced outside Africa (47.4%), 21.1 per cent at country specific levels and 5.3 per cent from other African countries.

From the students' perspective, in the context of indigenization of social work, 67.9 per cent of reference material used by social work students is from Europe and other developed countries, 17.2 per cent of the texts are from local publications, 13.5 per cent are texts from other African countries suggesting very limited use of locally produced material further making the indigenization process complex.

5.9 Areas for Improvement in the Social Work Education and Training

The overall aim at the end of this chapter is to assess whether there is a synthesis of material and content necessary for the training of social work in Kenya, and the level for effective training of social workers.

Social work educators may be preparing social workers for mainly generalist and community development work at the expense of the other approaches. This may, in a rather cyclic argument, explain why the level of policy making and advocacy may not be so high as these areas seem not to be emphasized in the curriculum. The research component has not been factored in, at all levels of training thus creating a disconnect in the imparting of analytical and problem assessment skills, to future practitioners.

In the context of indigenization, there seems not to be such a clear indicator of the direction to take. Indeed it seems that at the theoretical level, indigenization processes are supported but such support is missing at the practical level in terms of publishing, understanding and contributing to the debate from the educators and indeed, understanding the complexity of how the mechanisms to incorporate indigenization and the reality of actualizing. Most of the text materials are still from European countries, this implies that more needs to be done in terms of writing relevant material that clearly the address key issues of the indigenization process.

However, there is a general assertion from the students and practitioners that they are well prepared in terms of understanding poverty and also in realizing MDGs. This suggests a need for social work educational institutions to re-link with practitioners on a short course basis, to continue reviewing social work education goals in the context of changing challenges, and to ensure consistent engagement with the most current issues and how best to address them. If there is consistency of identification of areas that need to be improved on to ensure a dynamic social work education, and the practical enactment of such a process, then social work practitioners can attain the levels of social work education that will lead to poverty eradication and the attainment of Millennium Development Goals.

6

Challenges and Issues Confronting Social Work Clients

6.1 Problems Confronting Social Work Clients

Social work clients, sometimes referred to as the client system, are quite diverse. In Kenya, this ranges from the orphaned or neglected children, trafficked children, displaced families, drug food insecure stricken, groups, individuals and communities in different settings. In the study, social work practitioners indicated a wide range of problems, issues and challenges that often confront their clientele and which they commonly deal with in the course of their practice as indicated in Table 22.

Table 22: Social problems faced by clients

Problems	Frequency	Cumulative per cent
Poverty issues	139	68.8
Child neglect	112	55.4
Food insecurity	53	26.2
Illiteracy	45	22.2
Domestic violence	43	21.2
Poor health care	37	18.3
Lack of school fees	32	15.8
HIV/AIDS pandemic	25	12.3
Drug and substance abuse	16	7.9

Table 22 presents multiple responses, and indicates that poverty related issues were the commonest problems facing clients. It was rather surprising that child neglect featured so prominently, being reported by 55.4 per cent of the practitioners compared to, for instance, food insecurity which was identified by only 26.2 per cent of the practitioners. This has implications on the plight of the Kenyan child. Other problems identified were illiteracy, domestic violence, poor health care, lack of school fees, HIV/AIDS pandemic and drug abuse. It is worth noting that domestic violence was identified by 21 per cent of the respondents.

Besides these, other issues and challenges that often confront social work clients are directly related to their specific needs in the specific circumstances that they find themselves in. For example, clients who were ex-prisoners undergoing rehabilitation in Nakuru were experiencing diverse challenges in their efforts to settle down and fully integrate with the rest of the society. One observed...

'... we have no employment, there is no support from the government in providing sustainable support for ex-prisoners, there are no accessible micro finance opportunities, and the measures for acquiring a loan to start small business are stringent'.

However, they did not feel discriminated against by the rest in the society. Their main problem was how to make ends meet. One observed...

'... not anymore! We have been able to overcome the discrimination that executed earlier on especially when you are fresh from prison. Now we are able to freely interact with the rest of the community as normal people since we have reformed'.

In order to cope with life, they have joined hands and formed a group through which they get help from social workers in the Social Welfare Programme of the Catholic Diocese of Nakuru. The ex-prisoners did not have an idea of what professional social work is but knew what social workers do. They also felt that social workers are able to influence their well-being and satisfaction with life. Below are some of their observations. ...

'Social workers are the ones who assist the less privileged in society through offering counseling services and linking them to relevant resource agencies'.

'The social workers help us develop ideas on how to start income generating projects in the community and the women are encouraged to form groups which can be supported financially to start income generating activities such as rabbit keeping projects'.

Some other clients had an idea of who social workers are as long as they did something to benefit them. A client from the coast noted.....

'They are to help us be able to cope and make it easier to know what to do with our children. They have been instrumental in letting us have information such as even to visit this institution where we are receiving physiotherapy services for the children'.

It is important to note that in some situations, several challenges can compound the problems identified above. One such challenge has to do with access to services. While development organizations may have the resources and the personnel to deliver services to the needy, those targeted are often ignorant of how they can access such services. This is usually compounded by problems such as illiteracy, age and even gender. Besides, while some organizations have fairly elaborate and straight forward ways of offering services, others are viewed 'unfriendly'. In Kenya, where quite often those seeking services may have little formal education, such clients would avoid organizations where a lot of paperwork is involved or where the personnel look 'too sophisticated'. If clients feel out of place while seeking a service, they will only persevere if the service is not offered elsewhere.

The location of the service outlet equally matters. In Nairobi for instance, many NGOs are located in the most exclusive places, instead of having offices in the city center or in the slums where most of the disadvantaged live and therefore where they can be easily reached by those seeking their services. While some cite security as one of the determining factors for the choice of location; by so doing, they also limit access to their services. In the course of this study, one key informant was asked why her NGO was located 'away from where the needy are'. She argued that apart from security, 'too much access' would also be counterproductive as the needy were overwhelming in numbers. She argued that even when they 'hide', the needy somehow find them. The critical factor, she said, was services. She said that provided an organization was offering 'good services' to the clientele, it would matter very little where it is located. The needy, it would seem, have their own networks which they use to identify places where they can get services.

Another problem that clients face has to do with 'competing agencies'. In the arid and semi-arid lands (ASAL) of Kenya or in the city slums, you may find three or four development organizations offering more or less the same services, e.g. child sponsorship. This often sends the potential clients into a spin. They start comparing the services they offer, which organization is 'more generous', where could one access the services easily, etc. A family of a 'gatekeeper' therefore may have his/her three children sponsored by different organizations for comparison purposes or simply to take advantage of the available options. This will be to the disadvantage of another family that may have none of their children supported. Apart from the inherent problem of duplication of the services leading to wastage, these organizations cause a lot of confusion in the communities.

6.2   Desirable Social Changes in Society: Areas of Intervention for Social Workers

When social work practitioners were asked to identify some of the desirable social changes in the society, they mentioned economic stability, education for all, gender equity, access to health services, reduction in crime, food security, good governance and interethnic coexistence. Others desired a society that is drug free, has stable families and where child rights are protected.

Some of these desires are obviously part of the Millennium Development Goals (MDGs) and have been captured in the Kenya Vision 2030 and the Kenya Constitution, which are the blueprints for Kenya's future. The point of digression is that during the preparation of these important strategic documents, the voice of social workers seems to have been audible. One of the reasons has to do with lack of an organized mechanism to mobilize social workers. Given disorganization social workers have hardly any chance to influence decision making and policy. Although the Vision 2030 talks about the 'social pillar' as one of the three strategies of realizing the vision, social workers have neither been instrumental in drafting the contents of this pillar nor are they expected to play a critical role in its realization. Social workers, however, should not just cry foul as they have to fight for their relevance because the general society have no reason to involve social workers in endeavors they could benefit from if social workers allowed their course to be sidelined. Unfortunately, this should not be a competition of the professions because in the long run, it is the country that loses when the views of professional social workers are not sought when social work and social development frameworks are being crafted.

The frequent restructuring of government ministries often affects key issues of social work focus in the country. If previous experience is anything to go by, ministries such as Youth and Sports or Gender, Children and Social Development are often affected in the process of restructuring. This is because matters touching on 'social issues' are often not viewed as mainstream by government, hence the ministries identified above are easily subsumed in other ministries as departments. This would mean that matters touching on children, the youth, women, old people and the disabled among others are not given due preference in the allocation of resources. This is therefore an area that the social work fraternity in Kenya and beyond should watch closely. Social workers have to lobby members of parliament, other leaders, and bilateral as well as multilateral organizations on this cause.

It is hoped that with devolved government, the cash transfer programmes for OVCs and the elderly will be continued and expanded. It is also expected that programmes such as the Youth Enterprise Development Fund (YEDF) and the Women Enterprise Fund (WEF) would be expanded and well structured. The proposed Equalization Fund for marginalized areas needs to be closely monitored by social workers because in it lies the hope that previously underdeveloped areas will have a chance to catch up with the other areas. Of significance also is the requirement that in public appointments, no gender should constitute more than 66.6 per cent (2/3) of the establishment. This is particularly expected to benefit women who have previously been underrepresented in state jobs.

In the study, social work clients indicated several social changes that they desired to have in the society and which they believed social workers may help them achieve. A client from the coast observed that he needed...

'... a cohesive society, a well balanced person who has not been affected by the effects of drugs, a society that respects both men and women and does not allow patriarchy to abuse women, a society where education and gender equality is upheld'.

6.3   Experience of Social Work by Clients

From the colonial period, social work for many Kenyans is simply about assisting the poor by providing psychosocial support and material assistance. The mention of a social worker to many clients therefore evokes images of a perpetual giver or helper. And the 'giving' that is usually expected is material in nature, e.g., sponsorship for a child to pursue education, food relief during famine, provision of shelter and basic amenities during disasters, institutional care for an abandoned child and grants to self-help groups. Quite often therefore, if a social worker cannot give, then the client is disappointed. It has not helped that clients are used to the rehabilitative approach which unfortunately creates dependency. Clients therefore approach a social worker expecting to 'receive' or to be 'assisted' and not to participate in finding solutions to their own problems.

In the context of this study however, social work clients seemed to appreciate the role of social work in their lives. In Nakuru, they indicated that social workers had helped in rehabilitating them as noted in the following observation by a client who was an ex prisoner...

'Social workers have encouraged us in the fight against community stigmatization whereby before we were looked upon as outcasts by the community members, but now our self esteem is high and we can comfortably mix with the rest of the community members as normal people'.

Another social work client from the Solidarity with Women organization (SOLWODI) at the coast observed...

'We have been helped by social workers from Solidarity with Women in Distress who have listened and intervened in helping us to solve problems of women in distress. Having groups that are guided buy social workers has helped enhance the solidarity and understanding and helped us reform and join in the mainstream of everyday life'.

This brings to the fore the operations of Non Governmental Organizations, most of which have scope for social work services in Kenya. Some have their activities unregulated. There are, for instance, some that give handouts, creating dependency and setting a bad precedent for others. Since needy clients are often looking for short-term solutions to their afflictions, such NGOs are the darling of poor communities. NGOs that are professionally run, with relatively lengthy procedures on how clients can access services, and with certain work ethic are perceived to be insensitive by some clients. On the other hand, some clients prefer the services provided through NGOs than through other government agencies as observed by one client who stated as follows...

'... there is a difference in the way social workers do their work when they have been employed in the NGO sector and those in the government sector. The latter are less motivated and do not make enough follow-ups on cases and thus end up being ineffective, compared to those who work in the NGOs'.

From a critical perspective, other concerns may be noticeable. Quite often, there is ethnic discrimination in the service delivery. This occurs at two levels; where a development organization is dominated by a particular ethnic group in terms of personnel and two, where services are offered on the basis of ethnicity. This form of discrimination has also been witnessed in religious affiliation where a development organization appears to serve clientele from a particular faith.

Luckily, social work clients also know that not all their problems can be addressed. But this also places them in a perpetual state of anxiety. The fact that there are many needs and few resources to address them is something that clients come to terms with. Generally, many clients appreciate the work that NGOs do. Through civic education and other channels, many social work clients realize that it is first and foremost their own responsibility to meet their own needs and that as tax payers, they have a right to receive assistance from the government.

6.4 Culturally Sensitive Approach to Social Work Practice – Learning from the People Concerned

Social work practitioners acknowledged that in the course of their work at the grassroots level, they are often confronted with many culture related challenges. These, in most cases, revolve around issues that generally determine social lives and cultural practices. These include teenage/early marriages, child labor, polygyny, female circumcision, ethnic discrimination, religious differences, widow and property inheritance, patriarchy, gender based violence, language barriers and witchcraft. With 42 different ethnic groups in Kenya, social workers require competences that would enable them to work in diverse environments. Apart from embracing social work values such as 'acceptance' and 'self worth', social workers have to adopt a wide range of culturally sensitive approaches which in turn may strengthen their capacities and resolve to work with different client groups at the community level.

As a multidimensional discipline, social work borrows a lot from other disciplines. Of significance here is social/cultural anthropology, where social workers can learn about cultural diversity, belief systems, and rituals. While social workers should seek to understand Kenya's ethnic diversity and cultural practices, they have also to appreciate the fact that Kenya is changing fast and hence is in a cultural transition. There are Kenyans who have fairly conservative ideas either on the basis of ethnic values or religious orientation.

Owing to the fairly conservative nature of the Kenyan society, some social workers may find it difficult to accommodate those with 'different' sexual orientations notably transgender and homosexuals.

Most social workers are just as conservative as the rest of society and yet they are the ones who should champion tolerance and accommodation of these 'new' but assertive groups. So far, the Kenyan Government and the society in general have not been overtly anti-gay or transgender individuals as witnessed in Uganda and Zimbabwe. Nevertheless, the general attitude towards homosexuals and transgender persons is overwhelmingly negative. This is evident even at the university among social work students. For example, in one class of 30 social work students, just about 5 students appreciated the fact that there are gays in the Kenyan society and that these are normal human beings that should be accorded basic human rights of assembly and association. In nearly all cases, this small number of students will normally have an urban upbringing and would usually be from upper middle class families or higher. The positive attitude towards homosexuals and lesbians has a lot to do with the level of exposure to what are viewed as western values. The positive attitudes therefore have a lot to do with the neighborhood one grew up in, the schools attended and access to other socializing agents such as the electronic media.

One of the main reasons why about 30 per cent of Kenyans rejected the Kenya Constitution 2010 during the referendum, even with its entire popular reformist agenda, was because of certain clauses (e.g. the Bill of Rights) which were interpreted as implicitly allowing homosexuality and possibly same sex marriages. Besides, there are many Kenyans who voted for the adoption of the constitution in the hope that once adopted, certain changes would be made to explicitly outlaw such sexual orientations. There is a bit of disquiet in some of these conservative groups with some pointing out that the increased visibility of homosexuals in the print and electronic media has a lot to do with the Constitution.

It is important also to note that there are traditional practices that continue to evoke emotion in Kenya. Female genital mutilation or cutting remains a sensitive area of intervention. While the practice is illegal, it is commonly practiced in many communities in Kenya such as the Somali, Boran, Rendille, Kisii, Maasai and some sections of the Meru. While social workers working in these communities have to advocate for the rights of the girl-child, this has to be handled with caution and sensitivity to local values and practices. If such a worker is perceived to be out rightly against existing socio-cultural practices highly esteemed and cherished by the majority in the community, then that would make his/her work untenable. And yet on the other hand, it would be professionally unacceptable not to challenge the structures that perpetuate the practice.

Of equal concern are practices that affect women's development such as early marriages (e.g. among the Maasai, Samburu, Giriama and Digo communities) and wife-inheritance (e.g. among the Luo). Male circumcision, which is a common practice in Kenya, is a sensitive issue among the Luo where males are usually not circumcised. With clinical tests indicating that male circumcision reduces the chances of HIV transmission significantly (see O'Farrel and Egger, 2000), social workers are involved in the campaigns to popularize this practice in the Nyanza region. It is imperative that the social work training curricula has to be revised to accommodate some of these cultural issues that are extremely important in social work practice.

The culturally sensitive issues highlighted above are not only experienced by the clients and social work practitioners in different settings in Kenya but also by social work educators in training institutions as well. They reflect some of the ethical dilemmas that the said social work stakeholders go through in the course of their practice. The extent to which a social worker can isolate himself from what he believes is morally inappropriate as determined by the prevailing religious and cultural beliefs, and the demand for the profession to treat all individuals with utmost dignity, regardless of issues perceived to be morally inappropriate in such situations for example homosexuality, is a case in point. Nonetheless, all must render their services in the framework of the existing legal provisions and state statutes regarding such issues.

7

Gender and Social Development in the Context of Social Work in Kenya

7.1 Introduction

This chapter addresses gender issues in social work, paying particular attention to how the achievement of Millennium Development Goals (MDGs) has been contextualized within social work education, profession and service delivery in Kenya. This chapter draws from the primary data collected, with the aim of analyzing gender at local/agency and national level interventions in social work. A discussion regarding the nexus between gender and social work is generated, emphasizing the impacts of historical and cultural construction of gender on social work.

As part of the book, this section will provide students, educators and practitioners with an overview of how gender is integrated in the discipline of social work. It explores several dialogical ideas in order to enlighten future professional workers about the deeply gendered cultural meanings of the profession.

7.2 Social Work and Gender

Social work is a professional and academic discipline that seeks to improve the quality of life and wellbeing of an individual, group, or community. It functions by intervening through research, policy, community organizing, direct practice, and teaching on behalf of those afflicted with poverty or any real or perceived social injustices and violations of their human rights. There exists a strong linkage between social work and gender since most social problems experienced by men and women, boys and girls are systematically gendered. Gender refers to the relations between men and women, both perceptual and material. Gender is a central organizing principle of societies, and often governs the processes of production and reproduction, consumption and distribution. The gender perspective looks at the impact of gender on people's opportunities, social roles and interactions. Successful implementation of the policy, programme and project goals of international and national organizations is directly affected by the impact of gender and, in turn, influences the process of social development. Gender is an integral component of every aspect of the economic, social, daily and private lives of individuals and societies, and of the different roles ascribed by society to men and women.

Increasing evidence in Kenya reveals that while the very poor may have been lifted out of extreme poverty there has been a continuing rise in poverty.[7] The report draws attention to the problem of social segregation and shows that poverty is 'clustering' as the wealthy get wealthier. It also reveals that the gap between rich and poor is currently the highest it has been since independence. Poverty and inequality seem to be an intrinsic part of modern capitalism. Seemingly, poverty and inequality are the inevitable price to be paid when maintaining competitiveness in the global economy. The fact that wealth inequality continued to grow has caused public outrage. Protecting the advances that have already been towards gender equality, as well as accelerating and sustaining progress requires far-reaching changes. In the face of global shocks, crises and climate change, reducing the vulnerability of nations takes on renewed importance. In this context, social work as a profession as well as a practice should focus its poverty reduction efforts on supporting progress towards the achievement of universal blue prints such as the Convention on Elimination of Discrimination Against Women (CEDAW), MDGs and national plans such as Kenya's Vision 2030, making growth and development the work of everyone.

---

[7] Kenya Welfare Survey 2012.

7.2.1 Women and men in social work education

Study findings reveal that social work as an area of study is predominated by female students, where 71 per cent of students interviewed were female compared to 29 per cent male as indicated in Table 23.

Table 23: Per cent distribution of students by gender

Students	Frequency	Per cent
Male	62	28.8
Female	153	71.2
Total	215	100

These findings are characteristic of global trends because social work schools tend to be dominated by female students and faculty. This pattern is corroborated by the data derived from this study. To a large extent, these gender disparities have to do with the genesis of social work as a "helping activity". The social construction of gender roles tends to relegate the women to reproductive roles which are often characterized by "caring, helpful, voluntary and unpaid" work. In many societies, men and boys are socialized to engage in more "tough, aggressive, and non-tender or caring professions". It is at this point that gender becomes critical to social work. Career choice is influenced by gendered attitudes acquired or learnt through socialization. There are many important issues (such as the identity of the other and of ourselves) which we would like to encourage teachers of social work to problematize in the course of social work studies, because our understanding of the world around us depends on where we are positioned within it.

It is therefore no wonder that, in Kenya, every year a predominantly female and relatively homogenous group of young adults start their studies hoping to become qualified 'helpers' for other people who have faced problems in their lives. Initially, students tend to take for granted such matters as the present gender-based division of labor in the field of social care, and this easily leads them to reproduce the existing ways of working and of relating to each other in their respective communities.

7.3   Gender and Social Work Practice

Similar to the pattern among students, the disparity is still significantly higher among practitioners and employers where females are majority as indicated in Table 24.

Table 24:   Per cent distribution of practitioners by gender

Practitioners	Count	Per cent
Male	73	36.1
Female	129	63.9
Total	202	100

The fact that more female undergraduate social work students graduate from universities is a clear indication that there are more female practitioners compared to males.

Findings indicate that the main social work employment sectors include education 28 per cent, health 11 per cent, food security 5 per cent, community development 24 per cent, gender 1 per cent and other (child welfare protection and rehabilitation) 8 per cent. Since gender is cross-cutting, one of the major assumptions here is that all these employment sectors are in one way or the other addressing gender issues. Most of these sectors however are focused on addressing economic aspects of poverty by enabling communities to access material needs directly or indirectly; these typically including the necessities of daily living, such as food, clothing, shelter, or safe drinking water. Such social work practice is geared at enabling individuals and/ or communities address basic needs for a minimum standard of well-being and life, particularly as a result of a persistent lack of income.

Contemporary social issues are highly complex, globally interrelated, and dynamic. Social workers have contradictory roles when dealing with them: they have to act as instruments of government (the social control function) and as advocates of people oppressed by the policies of government and other authorities (the social change function). In the study, a range of gender based problems and issues handled by practitioners were found to revolve around poverty related issues of child neglect, food insecurity, illiteracy, domestic violence, poor health care, lack of school fees, HIV/AIDS pandemic and, drug and substance abuse.

An estimated 30 per cent of the practitioners in the study stated that poverty is the major problem facing their clients. Majority of the Kenyan poor are women as few of them access educational opportunities due to the low value placed on the girl child, as compared to the boy. Based on the traditional beliefs and practices, women have had less or no ownership, access and control to family assets and resources, as compared to males. In this respect, in the incidences of deprivation through poverty, females are more vulnerable.

Although deprivation for women and men is bad enough, for the former, it has a serious negative impact on the children because of the reduced performance in both reproductive and productive roles. Some of the key factors contributing to poverty include: precarious livelihoods, excluded locations, physical limitations, gender relationships, problems in social relationships, lack of security, abuse by those in power, disempowering institutions, limited capabilities and weak community organizations.

The government often assumes that social workers should deal with poverty without tackling the underlying causes. It continuously repeats the mantra of education as a panacea for all poverty and inequality and expects social workers to encourage children and adults to regard education as the main route out of poverty. The traditional social work role of striving to raise household incomes and improve housing conditions is often disregarded by government. Social workers must resist the notion that poverty can be tackled by apolitical social work solutions. They have a responsibility to work towards structural change to resolve the issues that their clients face which are caused by inequalities of income and wealth. It is not enough to simply resolve individual issues as they arise.

The pressures on social services departments in recent years have made it more likely that people in need do not receive adequate services. Social workers who find themselves in the situation of being unable to relieve hardship must understand the structural factors which exclude the poor from sharing in the lifestyles of the rest of society. These arise out of an economic system which exploits low paid workers and rewards the very rich. It is government action, rather than social work, that is needed to tackle growing inequality which is at the root of poverty.

7.4   Teaching Social Work from a Gender Perspective

The study reveals that most curricula from social work institutions has been under constant revisions with the aim of addressing emerging problem and issues particularly in response to MDGs. Gender equality and empowerment of women have been given priority as indicated in Table 25.

Gender is undoubtedly among the most important issues, owing to the fact that the worldview of women's views on family, child welfare, and parenting tend to become self-evident in the interactions between students and their teachers, and among peers. Without critical reflection on gender in everyday practices, social workers are likely to encourage the reproduction of traditional gender-specific family roles in circumstances in which adjustment to the changing world would be more appropriate. This has led the authors of this publication to make the following conclusion: it is not enough to question the present gendered practices of social work as such, but rather there is need to extend the investigation to some of the origins of the profession. It is important to acknowledge the particular gender order that existed when the earliest forms of the profession arose. Second, knowledge about how gender relations in general and the gendered practices of the profession in particular became established over time is a key aspect of the cultural heritage of the profession.

Table 25: MDGs receiving priority in your training programs

Social Issues receiving priority	Number of educators who responded	Per cent
Poverty reduction	16	32.7
Gender equality and empowering women	10	20.4
Education	6	12.2
Combat HIV/AIDS, malaria and other diseases	6	12.2
Environmental protection and sustainability	6	12.2
Maternal and child health	3	6.1
Global partnership for development	2	4.1
Total	49	100

7.5 Gender Equality in the Context of MDGs and Vision 2030

The Millennium Development Goal number 3 is to promote gender equality and empower women. Vision 2030 is Kenya's plan in spearheading social economic and political development. For social work professionals, it is clear that economic growth will not reduce poverty, improve equality and produce jobs unless its development frameworks are gender inclusive. Inclusive growth is also essential for the achievement of the other Millennium Development Goals (MDGs). From this perspective, inclusiveness means that men and women, boys and girls are involved in their social development process. This is in tandem with one of the key social work principles which perceive individuals as problem solvers.

Table 26: Roles that social work plays in the achievement of the MDGs

MDG areas targeted by social work programmes	Number of educators	Per cent
Empowerment on MDGs	40	38.8
Training of community members on IGAs	17	16.5
Networking with other agencies	10	9.7
Resource mobilization	9	8.7
Problem identification	7	6.8
Monitoring and evaluation of community projects	5	4.9
Educational support for children	4	3.9
Psychosocial support	3	2.9
Gender mainstreaming	3	2.9
Promotion of better health care services	3	2.9
Advocacy on human rights	2	1.9
Total	103	100

MDG 3 specifically provides that countries base policies on a comprehensive interpretation of women's empowerment. This includes support for programs aimed at helping women and men uncover, challenge and change traditions, policies, norms and attitudes that limit the lives of women and men during childhood, adolescence, child bearing and the rest of their lives and make long-term commitments to empower women and girls. Addressing deep-rooted issues of inequality, marginalization and discrimination is a long term process that involves social and structural change using the bottom-up approach. Governments and donors must be willing to support and sustain programmes aimed at empowering women and girls over a long-term time frame and support flexibility, learning and innovation.

In addition, creating supportive laws and policies, and ensuring their effective implementation is a requisite. Explicit laws and policies aimed at promoting women's and girl's rights are only meaningful if they are effectively implemented and enforced. Implementation requires mechanisms for accountability, including support for civil society engagement and advocacy to hold governments accountable, mobilize communities, and build coalitions to champion women's and girls' rights. The Constitution of Kenya (2010), Chapter 4, has taken into cognizance most of these fundamental rights.

Promoting gender equality also means engaging men and boys. Women's empowerment is not solely about them, nor can it be achieved by only engaging them. The engagement of men and boys is critical to achieving positive changes in the relationships and structures that shape the lives of women and girls as well as those of men and boys. Incorporating gender analysis and women's empowerment objectives into programming is critical. Governments, development agencies and civil society actors should conduct gender analyses as part of all programming with the goal of identifying and addressing gender inequities and barriers. Key efforts include: collection of gender disaggregated data and integrating women's needs and perspectives into program design, implementation, monitoring and evaluation. Supporting social networks and safe spaces for women and girls is also a concern for social workers. Providing women and girls with a space to build legitimacy and support is an important step in reducing their isolation, and encouraging their participation, collective action and empowerment. Such spaces may include savings and loans groups for women and social networks and clubs for girls. The study confirms that social workers are actively involved in these activities.

7.6   Social Work and Social Development

Social equity and equitable access to public services have been part of the nation's development agenda since independence. However, concerns have been raised on the extent of the disparities between the rich and poor and inequitable distribution of public resources between individuals, regions and along gender lines. There are also rural urban inequalities, income disparities within the rural areas themselves and within major cities and towns. Moreover, an increasing number of urban residents live in informal settlements lacking the most basic amenities. Such disparities, which include issues of quality, have been a major cause of social tensions in the country as was evident during the 2007 post-election crisis. Inequality and poverty therefore remain among the key development challenges that the government continues to confront and address. Whereas substantial attention has been placed on poverty alleviation, there exists a huge gap between the poor and the non-poor in the entitlement to political, civil and human rights. There also exists large disparities in incomes and access to education, health and land, as well as to basic needs, including; clean water, adequate housing and sanitation. In addition, there exist other remarkable intra-regional, inter-regional, and gender disparities in poverty and inequality levels.

To say that this study indicates a salient level of involvement by social workers in alleviating underdevelopment and suffering is not to undermine the usefulness of this prestigious profession in the future of Kenya. Social workers, for example, in their practice have been actively contributing to the national key programmes aimed at reducing poverty and inequalities by 2012 as outlined in Vision 2030. The involvement of social work and social workers is critical towards achieving a socially equitable and just society. Social work has a role in supporting the government to implement policies and programmes that minimize the differences in income opportunities and access to social services across Kenya's geographical regions, paying special attention to the most disadvantaged communities in the Arid and Semi-Arid Districts, urban informal settlements and pockets of poverty in high potential areas. That means that social workers will be involved in increasing community empowerment through monitoring and management of "devolved" public funds for both social and income programmes. Only social workers can ensure that the allocations to these funds will be in favor of the most disadvantaged communities and areas since they operate within an ethical framework of principles and values.

There is growing recognition internationally that gender equality is good for economic growth and essential for poverty reduction (Ellis 2004). Where gender inequalities constitute barriers to women entering or participating fully in markets, economic growth and private sector development will be constrained with less investment, less competition, and lower productivity (Blackden and Bhanu 1999). Although the government of Kenya's Economic Recovery Strategy for Wealth and Employment Creation 2003–2007 recognizes that women have unequal access to opportunities and assets, it does not examine the implications of this inequality (Government of Kenya 2003).

For Kenya, Klasen (2002) reveals that the fact that women during the 1960–92 period did not complete as many years of schooling on average as men did accounts for the almost 1 percentage point difference between the long-run growth potential of Kenya when compared with that of high performing Asian economies (with long-run growth rates of 4.5%). In Kenya, economic analysis therefore suggests that eliminating gender-based inequalities in education and access to agricultural inputs could result in a one-off increase in output by as much as 4.3 percentage points of GDP, followed by a sustained year-on-year increase of 2.0 to 3.5 percentage points in GDP growth.

The prevalence of HIV/AIDS in Kenya is higher for women than for men, with infection rates for females in the 15 to 19 age range being a staggering five times higher than for males (World Bank 2004a, KDHS 2008/09). The increasing number of widows and orphans resulting from the high number of HIV/AIDS cases has significantly increased women's workload and their financial responsibilities (NACC 2011). Growing evidence indicates that gender-based violence contributes to the higher infection rates for women. Other reasons include traditional norms and cultural practices, as well as women's economic dependence on men (World Bank 2004). HIV/AIDS is also having an impact on land rights for women who are already insecure.

The Kenyan Strategic Country Gender Assessment reports that 24 per cent of women in the country have been victims of rape. Perpetrators are listed as male household staff, neighbors, ex-husbands, employers or supervisors, and landlords (World Bank 2004). In 2002, 60 per cent of married women in Kenya reported that they were victims of domestic violence, and 83 per cent of women reported physical abuse in childhood, with more than 60 per cent reporting physical abuse as adults (Johnston 2002a, 2002b). Under customary law, a man beating up his wife can be considered reasonable chastisement and may therefore take place with impunity.

Kenya's national gender policy is instrumental in the realization of social work goals. The policy aims at: creating an enabling policy environment for translating government commitment to gender equality into a reality; establishing policies, programmes, structures and mechanisms to empower women and men to transform gender relations in all aspects of work, at all levels of government as well as within the broader society; ensuring that gender considerations are effectively integrated into all aspects of government policies, activities and programmes; establishing an institutional framework for the advancement of the status of women as well as the achievement of gender equality; and advocating for the promotion of new attitudes, values and behavior, and a culture of respect for all human beings in line with the new policy and represent a significant step in the continued struggle for gender equality and justice in Kenya by enhancing the visibility and influence of the National Gender Machinery.

A greater emphasis on understanding how gender stereotyping in the social work profession influences decision making right from recruiting students into the social work programs, students attitudes towards social work as a 'woman's field' and difficulties faced by female faculty in accessing publishing and subsequent promotion opportunities is required. Since poverty has gender dimension, most service delivery systems tend to serve women and girls.

Though some social work training institutions are already offering gender studies, it is imperative that this trend, through existing coordinating mechanisms for university education be made universal. Social work should embrace gender as a critical factor which leads to inequality and poverty.

Persons responsible for revising curricula as well as scheduling regular faculty and administrative work to review existing gender disparities should act to influence faculty hiring, promotion, job duties, and the distribution of resources. Accumulating advantage by gender occurs on a variety of levels from differential promotions, salary, job assignments, and resources (e.g. office space, course releases, and overall salary differences, and discretionary funds) – all of which must be transparent, systematically monitored, and open for discussion if social work programs are to remain strong. Social workers must be willing to actively engage in practices that support the profession's stated goals, values, and ethics related to social justice and equity, which requires a willingness to monitor and change every day practices and policies that disadvantage women. When educators do not model a commitment to social and economic justice, students note the disparity and hypocrisy between social work rhetoric and reality.

8

Recommendations and Conclusion

8.1 Introduction

This chapter briefly highlights the key recommendations derived from the study findings that should be prioritized for a much stronger social work profession in Kenya. The recommendations revolve around the three levels within which different stakeholders facilitate and strengthen professional social work operations namely: training, practice and policy. It is worth mentioning that some of the recommendations are intertwined and cut across the three levels. Specific modalities to make each of the recommendations practical should be considered and worked around the three levels.

8.2 Recommendations for Poverty Reduction and Realization of MDGs at Training Level

Given that the time lines set for the achievement of the Millennium Development Goals (MDGs) are almost over, there is need to have the key lessons learnt through the MDGs incorporated into the social work curriculum in different institutions. Most of them are still relevant and have a bearing on social issues which affect people in different ways.

Social work curriculum in the training institutions must also be revised on regular basis in order to flow with the changes in current social issues that affect different client groups. Equally important here is to ensure a critical shift from heavy reliance on social work ideals from the west to more indigenized ideals that are practically relevant to local situations and which both practitioners and their clients can easily identify with. Post graduate social work education in both Masters and PhD level must also be considered in line with the trends in place for other social sciences. This will immensely help boost up advanced social work skills in research, case assessment, case management and other areas of social work interventions.

Holistic training of social work students must also be prioritized particularly with regard to supervised field education in all levels of training. A serious concern was noted where social work academic staff are unable to supervise their students directly while in their field practicums owing to different reasons including the failure by social work institutions to meet the supervisor's financial expenses in the field.

Additionally, field education must be well planned and coordinated such that a student is aware, well in advance about the dates and duration for field work in order to allow quality time in the choice of field placement agency and subsequent orientation about its focus and services offered. This in turn will adequately prepare the hosting agency well in advance for the incoming student thus strengthening the agency-student relationship during the internship period.

More lecturers trained and qualified in social work must also be hired and provided with relevant updated social work reference materials. They must also be challenged to undertake social work research on a regular basis and engage more in depth interactions with practicing social workers on the ground. This will ensure a spontaneous flow of information and knowledge development on issues related to social work between social work educators and practitioners. Most importantly, it will greatly contribute to the integration of theory and practice hence fresh social work graduates will not experience the frustrating reality that currently exists where they find severe variations in social work theory and practice in the field.

The government must also play an active role in ensuring that appropriate standards for social work education and practice are set and adhered to both in social work training institutions as well as the social work agencies. This entails accrediting social work institutions and recognition of social work as a profession by the government through enactment of legislative measures for social work education and practice. If done, this has the potential to make the voice of social work more vibrant for social work personnel in the training institutions and in the practice.

8.3 Recommendations for Poverty Reduction and Realization of MDGs at Practice Level

These recommendations are mainly centered on agencies that collaborate with social work training institutions for social work field education, social work practitioners and the Government. They point to the need for a vibrant social work voice through a united social work forum to spearhead the changes needed in social work practice at the grass root level.

Efforts in poverty reduction must not be left to the government alone but must also be spearheaded by all social work stakeholders in the agencies where social work is practiced. These agencies should then adopt and incorporate MDGs in their programmes given their different focus in terms of their vision and mission. Prioritization of certain aspects of MDGs will nonetheless make a big difference in facilitating their realization at practice level.

Development agencies must also be encouraged to employ qualified professional social workers who must adhere to a professional social work code of ethics in their practice. The development of such a code must be embarked on immediately by all social work stakeholders. This would make a big difference in terms of putting in place appropriate standards for social work practice and also inculcate a strong feeling of comradeship among social work practitioners.

Community participation must also be further consolidated in all policy measures undertaken to deal with poverty both at policy and the practice level. This is because community members are critical stakeholders whose involvement or the lack of it has the potential to enhance such measures or otherwise. Equally important is the need to remunerate social work practitioners with improved service benefits and salaries to avoid heavy turnovers for employees which sometimes affects the programmes in place or those starting.

8.4 Recommendations for Poverty Reduction and Realization of MDGs at Policy Level

Clear principles to guide the decisions and to achieve rational outcomes need to be put in place to ensure that poverty is reduced and that MDGs are realized. Moreover, an implicit intent and procedural strategy for implementation have to be out in place. This requires concerted effort amongst all specified stakeholders particularly in the formulation and influencing of policies that will make the social work profession visible and recognized in agencies that hire professional social work services and among other professions as well.

At the level of formulation of policies, stakeholders need to identify the gaps that exist in both training and practice of professional social workers. Specifically, a thorough examination of the content and consistency or variance in training *vis a vis* the final qualifications and knowledge that social work students should end up with to build their capacity to contribute to eradication of poverty and realization of MDGs is critical. The role of key educational ministries and relevant commissions such as the Commission for University Education in such policy formulation is critical.

It is necessary to have in place a professional body to regulate social work practice by overseeing and assessing the trained social work professionals to ensure they are up to the task. Such a body could also offer targeted professional programmes to cater for any shortfall and be mandated to offer certificates of practice to confirm adherence to the adequate training on completion of social work courses in all institutions that offer social work training. Such a regulatory framework will assess and help streamline the accreditation of institutions offering social work and ensure that they meet global standards for social work education in terms of qualified human resources, content, handing of field work and internship programmes.

One of the important findings from the research is that the involvement of especially educators in policy making is low. The educators have the necessary knowledge and hands on experience that can be utilized in policy formulation and implementation, and therefore a policy requirement for their involvement in policymaking at national level is important.

Clear policy that provides guidelines regarding the working environment required for effective and ethical social work practice, alignment of organizational, and social work practice objectives also need to be developed in collaboration with Government.

The context for practice varies according to local circumstances and local practice is guided by local and national policies and guidelines. This necessitates coming up with policies and guidance for employers and agencies that need to be published by national regulatory bodies. There is therefore need for consistent effort to improve the laws, regulations and organizational policies which affect social welfare policy and social work practice. This entails formulating policies for the protection of the interests of service users, promotion of good standards of practice and quality services, improved healthcare for all, addressing learning disabilities, enhancing high quality care for all, information sharing and improved mental health initiatives. These policies can be needs oriented and achieved by putting in place joint strategic needs assessment between key social work organizations, programmes and service departments to ensure targeted populations have poverty reduced and MDGs realized.

8.5 Way Forward and Conclusion

Considering the fact that the time set by the United Nations Organization for the implementation of Millennium Development Goals is now almost over, the PROSOWO research team in Kenya is hopeful that the lessons learnt and the gains made with regard to the realization of MDGs should not end within the given time span. Social work educators and social work practitioners alike still have more work to do to ensure that these gains are consolidated in social work training and practice with additional effort made for their sustainability. This calls for close working relations with all cadres of social workers and streamlining of structures to support such effort.

The recommendations on social work education, strategies and to make it workable will be worked out and tabled to respective departments and university structures for consideration and ease of implementation. It is hoped that other universities in Kenya may see the need to incorporate the same recommendations. In this regard, the PROSOWO study findings and subsequent recommendations will be presented to all universities that have social work training programmes in the country. In addition, the report will be shared with the Council for University Education in Kenya with the hope that the council will consider the recommendations therein in the process of accrediting social work education programmes at university level.

References

Abagi, O. and Olweya, J. (1999). *Educational reform in Kenya for the next decade: Implementing policies for adjustment and revitalization.* Institute of Policy Analysis Research, Nairobi.

Abbot, A. (2002). *Measuring social work values: A cross cultural challenge for global practice.* International Social Work, 42(4).

Abbot, A. (1988*). Professional choices: values at work.* National Association of Social Workers, Silver Springs MD.

Agresti, A. (1990). *Categorical data analysis.* John Wiley and Sons, New York.

Agresti, A. and Finlay, B. (1997). *Statistical methods for the social sciences.* Prentice Hall, New Jersey.

Banks, S. (2001). *Ethics and Values in Social Work.* Macmillan Press, London.

Barkan, J.D. and Chege, M., (1989). *Decentralizing the state: District focus and the politics of reallocation in Kenya. The Journal of Modern African Studies*, Vol. 27, No. 3 (Sep., 1989), pp. 431–453.

Barretta-Herman, A. (2005). *A reanalysis of the IASSW World Census 2000.* International Social Work, 48(6).

Blackden, C. and Bhanu, C. (1999). *Gender, growth, and poverty reduction. Special program of assistance for Africa.* 1998 Status Report on Poverty in Sub-Saharan Africa; World Bank Technical Paper no. 428; Washington DC.

Blackden, C.M., S. Canagarajah, S. Klasen, and D. Lawson (2006). *Gender and growth in sub-Saharan Africa: issues and evidence.* Research Paper 2006/37, 107.

Bellù, L.G. and Liberati P. (2005). *Impacts of policies on poverty: The definition of poverty*, FAO, Rome.

Chitere, O. and Ireri, O.N. (2004). "District focus for rural development in Kenya: its limitations as a decentralization and participatory planning strategy and prospects for the future", Institute of Policy Analysis and Research, Nairobi.

Delgado, M. (2000). *Community social work practice in an urban context: the potential of a capacity enhancement perspective.* Oxford University Press, Oxford.

Ellis, J. (2004). *Preventing violence against women and girls: A study of educational programmes for children and young people.* London: WOMANKIND Worldwide.

Ergas, Z.R. (1982). *Kenya's special rural development program (SRDP): Was it really a failure? The Journal of Developing Areas*, Vol 17, pp 51–66.

Gray, Mel & Fook, Jan. 2004. *The quest for a universal social work: Some issues and implications.* Social Work Education 2004, Volume 23 No. 5.eISSN: 1470–1227.

Garber, R. (2000). *Social work and globalization. Canadian Social Work Journal.*

Ganayake, S. and Ganayake, J. (1988). *Training manual for community workers.*

Gray, Mel (2006). *The progress of social development in South Africa. International Journal of Social Welfare*, 15 (Supplement 1):S53–S64.

Grusec, J.E. and Lytton, H. (1988). *Social development: History, theory and research.* New York, NY, US: Springer-Verlag Publishing.

GOK (2012). *Government of the Republic of Kenya. Kenya Welfare Survey,* Ministry of Planning and National Development, Nairobi.

GOK (2012). *Revised National Policy on Gender and Development.* Ministry of Gender, Children and Social Development, Nairobi.

GOK (2011). *Fund Status Report.* Ministry of Youth and Sports, Nairobi.

GOK (2010). *Constitution of Kenya, 2010.* Kenya Gazette Supplement, Government Printer, Nairobi.

GOK (2010). *Kenya 2009 Population and Housing Census Report.* Kenya National Bureau of Statistics, Nairobi.

GOK (2008). *2008/09 Kenya Demographic and Health Survey.* Kenya National Bureau of Statistics, Nairobi

GOK (2008). *Medium Term Plans 2008–2012.* Ministry of Planning and National Development, Nairobi.

GOK (2007). *Kenya Vision 2030, A Globally Competitive and Prosperous Kenya.* Government of the Republic of Kenya, Nairobi.

GOK (2002). *Perspectives of the Poor on Anti-poverty Policies in Selected Districts.* Kenya Participatory Impact Monitoring, Human Resources and Social Services Department, Nairobi.

GOK (2003a). *Economic Recovery Strategy for Wealth and Employment Creation 2003–2007.* Ministry of Planning and National Development, Nairobi.

GOK (2000a). *National Policy on Gender and Development.* Ministry of Planning and National Development, Nairobi.

GOK (2000b). *Second Report on Poverty in Kenya, Vol. II.* Ministry of Planning and National Development, Nairobi.

GOK (1999). *National Micro and Small Enterprise Baseline Survey. Central Bureau of Statistics.* Ministry of Planning and National Development Nairobi.

Healy, L.M. and Link, R.J. (2012). *Handbook of international social work: Human rights, development and global professions.* Oxford University Press, Oxford.

Heofer, R. (2006). *Advocacy practice for social justice.* Lyceum Press, Chicago.

Human Rights Watch, (2003). *Double standards: women's property rights violations in Kenya.* Human Rights Watch, New York.

Ife, J. (2002). Human rights and social work: towards rights based approach. University of Cambridge Press, New York.

International Association of Schools of Social Work (IASSW), 2014. *Global definition of the social work profession,* in http://www.iassw-aiets.org acessed on 20th May 2014.

International Federation of Social Workers (IFSW), (2014). *Global definition of the social work profession,* in http://www.ifsw.org accessed on 20th May 2014.

Johnston, T. (2002a), *Domestic abuse in Kenya.* Nairobi: Population Communications Africa.

Johnston, T. (2002b), *Violence and abuse of women and girls in Kenya.* Population Communications Africa.

Kenyatta University (2005). *The role of African universities in the attainment of Millennium Development Goals.* Kenyatta University, Nairobi.

Kettner, P.M., Netting, F.E. and McMurtry, S.L. (1993). *Social work macro practice.* New York: Longman.

Klasen, S. (2002). *Low schooling for girls, slower growth for all? Cross-Country evidence on the effect of gender inequality in education on economic development.* John Hopkins University Press, Baltimore.

Klasen, S. and F. Lamanna. (2003). *The impact of gender inequality in education and employment on economic growth in the Middle East and North Africa.* Background paper, World Bank, Washington DC. In http://www.iai.wiwi. uni- goettingen.de/ klasen/klasenlamanna.pdf accessed on 20th May 2014.

Leys, C. (1975). *Under-development in Kenya.* East African Publishers, Nairobi.

Lundi, C. (2006). *Social work's commitment to social justice: A challenge to the profession.* In Social Work: Making a World of Difference, Hall, N. (eds). International Federation of Social Workers and Fafo.

Lombard, A. (2007). *The impact of social welfare policies on social development in South Africa: An NGO perspective.* Social Work/Maatskaplike Werk, 43(4):295–316.

Lombard, A. and Wairire G.G. (2010*). Developmental social work in South Africa and Kenya: Some lessons for Africa.* In *The Social Work Practitioner-Researcher,* University of Johannesburg, March 2010.

Mupedziswa, R. (1997). *Training social workers in an environment of economic reforms: The "mother" of all challenges?"* Social Work/Maatskaplike Werk , vol. 33, no. 3.

O'Farrell, N. and Egger M. (2000). *Circumcision in men and the prevention of HIV infection: A 'meta-analysis' revisited.* In *J STD AIDS,* 11(3):137–42.

Onyango, V. and Schmidt, M. (2008). *Poverty and disease remediation in the Millenium Development Goals: Time for Kenya to set standards and thresholds?"* In M. Schmidt, J. Glasson, L. Emmelin and H. Helbron (eds.), Standards and

Thresholds for Impact Assessment, Cottbus: Springer-Verlag. Pp. 49–62.

Roche, C. (2004). *Impact assessment for development agencies: learning to value change.* "Oxfam, London.

Rothman, J. (1996). *The interweaving of community intervention approaches. Journal of Community Practice.*

Sen A. (1985). *Commodities and capabilities.* North-Holland, Amsterdam, The Netherlands.

Sewpaul, V. (2001). *Models for intervention for children in difficult circumstances in South Africa. Child Welfare Journal,* 80(5 September/October).

Tripod, T. and Potocky-Tripodi, M. (2007). *International social work research: Issues and prospects.* Oxford University Press, Oxford.

UNDP (2011). *Human development report 2011: Sustainability and equity: a better future for all.* New York.

USAID (2009). *Achieving the MDGs: the contribution of family planning in Kenya* - USAID Policy Initiative.

Wairire, G.G. (2008). *The challenge for social work in the Kenyan context of political conflict,* (Book Chapter 5, Pgs 101-122) in Shula Ramon (Eds), Social Work Facing Political Conflict, Venture Press, London.

Weaver, H.N. (2006). *Social work through an indigenous lens: reflections on the state of our profession.* In Social Work: Making a World of Difference, Hall, N. ed.

Weil, M.O. (1996). *Model development in community practice: A historical perspective. Journal of Community Practice.*

World Bank (2004a). *From periphery to centre: A strategic country gender assessment.* PREM and ESSD, Africa Region, World Bank, Washington, DC.

World Bank (2004b). *Impact of international trade on gender equality,* Notes 86, World Bank, Washington, DC.

World Bank, *Economic adjustment in Sub-Saharan Africa.* Technical Note 13, Poverty and Human Resources Division, Africa Region, Washington, DC.